The PERSON Inside

THIS WOMAN'S JOURNEY TO WHOLENESS

Myra H. Doyle

ISBN 979-8-89243-064-7 (paperback)
ISBN 979-8-89243-065-4 (digital)

Christian Faith Publishing
832 Park Avenue
Meadville, PA 16335
www.christianfaithpublishing.com

Printed in the United States of America

To Judy J. and in memory of Marie and my beloved husband, Kenneth.

Contents

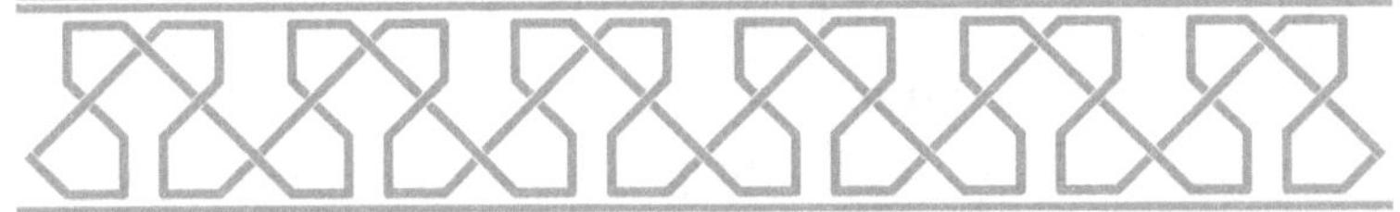

Introduction

Many people grow up in dysfunctional or abusive homes. The dysfunction and abuse can come in many forms and at many levels of severity. Mistreatment can wreak havoc with a child's mind, emotions, and even their body, often leaving visible and invisible scars. And the memories can not only last a lifetime but actually disable the victim. There are survivors who actually feel the sting of a smack or a slap or a whack of a wooden paddle to their backsides decades later.

Child abuse is a form of rejection. The child wasn't the gender the parent wanted, or the child was unplanned, or the child just isn't the way the parent wants them to be. Sometimes the abuse is directed toward the innateness of the child, the naturalness of the child, something God put in the child to make them unique.

Rejection is probably the most common form of child abuse. And from my own experience, the most personal. It rebukes, censures, restricts, or represses the naturalness of the child—the *person* of the child. Therefore, the intolerance of certain qualities or characteristics of the child goes straight to the spirit, the core of who we are. We are a spirit, we have a soul which consists of our emotions and attitudes, and we have a mind where we reason and think.

Spiritual deliverance in the name of Jesus is the only way out of the darkness that has encompassed you. It is the only way to undo the damage that was done to you as a child.

Maybe you are a battered spouse. The same principle applies because spousal abuse is another form of rejection and, likewise, can do a lot of damage to the heart of the victim. Spiritual deliverance allows God to enter the damaged areas and bring healing and restoration.

Deliverance is actually casting out demonic spirits that can enter the victim's soul—as opposed to the spirit—which they cannot have access to because that's where God resides. (God and demons cannot cohabitate. Neither one will tolerate existing with the other.) Any kind of abuse can open a door to demonic forces. If you constantly heard criticism as a child or a spouse, and you believed the negative words spoken over and to you, as I did, you caused the demons inadvertently to enter your soul. You gave them access because you accepted the hateful, critical words spoken and believed them. The demonic spirits came in through your ears on those words. When we listen to negative or encouraging words, we choose to accept the words about us. In a battery situation, the offender is usually someone we trust so we accept their words that describe us. Only God through the name of Jesus can expel the demonic spirits. After deliverance comes inner healing. You can't receive healing first because the demonic forces won't allow it. You must get rid of them first.

I am not a psychologist, psychiatrist, or therapist, nor am I an emotional or mental counselor of any kind. I am a survivor of child abuse. I was physically and psychologically abused to the point of suicide. But I experienced spiritual deliverance on many occasions by ministers of deliverance.

This book was conceived to kindle hope in the hearts of readers who need deliverance and inner healing so that they, too, can experience freedom, healing, restoration, peace, hope, joy, and purpose.

God has an intent and a design for each of our lives. A particular goal or expectation, a calling, that only we can fulfill. Deliverance and inner healing allow us the opportunity to discover our God-given plan and purpose and empower us to achieve that calling.

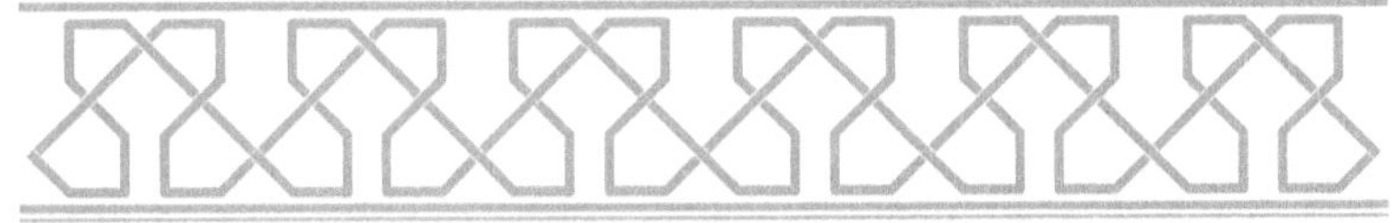

My Beginning

G OD KNEW US before we were born.

> For I know the plans I have for you,
> declares the Lord, plans for welfare and
> not evil, to give you a future and a hope.
> (Jeremiah 29:11 TLB)

> Before I formed you in the womb I knew
> you, and before you were born I conse-
> crated you; I appointed you a prophet to
> the nations. (Jeremiah 1:5 TLB)

We aren't all called to be a prophet, but we all have a
God-given purpose to fulfill until He calls us home.

> For we are His workmanship, created in
> Christ Jesus for good works, which God
> prepared beforehand, that we should
> walk in them. (Ephesians 2:10 NASB)

No one is a mistake. No one is an accident. No one is
the wrong gender. No one is useless to God, unaccepted by
Him, or a surprise to Him.

I am a survivor of child abuse. I was born into a very
strict, Christian, major denominational church family. My

mother was a mild-mannered, quiet, warm, loving, Proverbs 31 woman, every inch a lady. My father, on the other hand, was anxious, pessimistic, controlling, and a worrier who always believed he knew best.

My parents wanted two children—a boy and a girl. Before the time my mother was carrying me and my twin sister, a daughter had been born. She was seventeen months older than my twin sister and me. After the doctor noted two heartbeats, my father began to worry about how they were going to take care of three children. Knowing my father, I believe he worried about the issue day and night, never hesitating to share his worries with my mother. Therefore, while in my mother's womb, I knew that someone out there didn't want me. I believe that I knew, even then, that I was the second of a pair of twins. I've heard and read stories where twins reached for each other when laid side by side, so they know that they were not alone while in their mother's womb.

My sister was born five minutes before I was. Could it be that because of my fear of the person "out there," I hesitated, I stalled my delivery? I think so. The nurse kept repeating, "I can't hear the other heartbeat," over and over. In my teens, I wished she never did. We were exactly four weeks early. I was weak and needed extra care for the first couple of months of my life. Maybe that had a part in my father's opinion of me. Maybe he thought I was a weakling and a burden. So not being a son he so badly wanted, and being a third child he felt like he could not afford, needing extra attention, and perhaps believing that I wasn't as smart or quick-minded as my twin sister all added to his displeasure toward me.

> For You formed my inward parts. You covered me in my mother's womb. I will praise You for I am fearfully and wonderfully made. Marvelous are Your

works. And that, my soul knows very
well. My frame was not hidden from you
when I was made in secret. And skillfully
wrought in the lowest part of the earth.
Your eyes saw my substance, being yet
unformed. And in Your book they all
were written, the days fashioned for me,
when as yet there were none of them.
(Psalm 139:13–16 NKJV)

God knew us before our conception and has a plan for
each one of us.

I knew that my mother loved me. She always had time
for each of her three daughters. When one of us needed
attention, we would go to her while she was busy keeping
house, and she would hug us, kiss us, and stroke our hair.
And she would speak to us in a soft, gentle voice. I felt safe
when I was close to her. I felt accepted as I was. I felt like I
was okay as a person.

When we were almost five years old, as our mother
watched out the window for our sister to walk across the
field from school to the back of our house, my twin sister
suggested that we climb into the grass-green vinyl platform
rocker, with wooden arms covered in the green vinyl by little
brass tacks, turn sideways, and drop onto the floor on our
bottoms. Mother would turn to look at us and just laugh.
We climbed into that rocker three or four times, with mother
laughing, standing two feet away, when my father came rush-
ing in from the kitchen where he was having coffee. He commanded, "Stop that! Get down! You're going to tear up that
chair!" He scolded us, pointing his finger at me, and telling
us that we were too loud, and we had to calm down. I trem-
bled. Even then, I knew he was mostly referring to me.

My sister took my left hand and said, "Come on, My (pronounced Mye). Let's go outside." That's one incident I recall so vividly.

The things we did where we got in trouble were not things that were wrong. They were things that annoyed or irritated my father. They were things all children do as children because they *are* children. Children don't think like adults, and my father expected us to behave like adults. He expected us to sit quietly at the kitchen table at meal times. No laughing. No carrying on. Every now and then, I would catch his stare, and I would melt. My father was always a no-nonsense person. He hated it when my twin and I "carried on." He hated when we were in the living room being rowdy in play, giggling all through it. He constantly told us, especially me, to be quiet, that I was too loud. All the while, my mother was enjoying our fun and laughter.

When he would scold me, even as a young child, he was always angry. He never just said, "Stop that, honey." My twin sister would watch with eyes wide. Even though my sister and I were doing the same things, making the same noise, my father would point me out. Apparently, I was the *chosen one*.

Before my twin sister and I started first grade, my father concluded that there was something wrong with me intellectually. I was defective. He believed I was mentally deficient. He insisted that my mother take me to a psychologist to have my intelligence tested, and my acuity measured. I remember getting in a cab and asking my mother where we were going. She just replied, "To the doctor."

After the testing, the doctor told me to play with some toys and games on the floor while she talked to my mother. I heard her say, "There's nothing wrong with your daughter." (I'm so glad I heard the doctor say that.) I don't know how my father reacted. I'm sure he thought the doctor was mistaken. From that time on, he was convinced that I had limited intelligence and eventually he would begin to tell me that on a regular basis. And I began to believe him.

My twin sister and I played with our dolls, inside games, and what we called *playing house*. Sometimes we played school with our older sister. On warm sunny days, my twin sister and I liked playing outdoors. We played yard games alone or with the other kids in the neighborhood. Some of those games were freeze, tag, Simon Says, Mother May I, Red Light-Green Light, jacks, and our favorite, hopscotch. We played ball and ran races. We climbed trees. When I think back, I'm surprised we were allowed to climb trees for fear of falling out of one. Any of these activities could cause me to get in trouble. Even running and laughing could get me in trouble because my father feared I would fall down and get hurt, and when I did get hurt, like a scraped knee or elbow, he would scold me. "See? I told you not to run!" My sister was not scolded for running. I guessed because she didn't fall and scrape herself. So I reasoned that I was being punished for getting hurt, not for running. Often, when I got injured playing outside with my sister, I was scolded, my wound treated, and commanded to sit on the couch until told I could leave.

One day, my clever sister suggested that we sit on the top step of the staircase and bounce down, hitting each step with our bottoms. Believe it or not, it was so much fun. She went first, as usual. On my second or third trip down, my father came to the staircase because of all our giggles, I suppose, and found me almost halfway down. He was not happy. Actually, he was angry. I don't think I got a whipping for it, but I sure got a scolding. As usual, my twin would say, "Come on, My. Let's…" whatever. Often, when I got a scolding or a whipping, it was because of the results of what I was doing.

My father always explained a potential, drastic, negative scenario that my actions would cause that would cost money to repair or replace, or it would leave us without something that we needed. Pouring a glass of milk while the refrigerator door was open would cause all the food to spoil. Likewise, refilling an ice tray while the door was open would do the same. Being rowdy in a chair would tear it up, and it would have to be replaced, and he didn't have the money to buy another one. Running under the clothesline, lined with laundry, would tear it down, and everything on the clothesline would either have to be re-laundered or replaced. He stressed to me all the reasons my actions were unacceptable but always in an angry raised voice. He never calmly explained to me why certain actions were not acceptable, like my mother did, and why not do them without getting angry and scolding me. He seemed to believe that I should know all the repercussions of my carelessness. Maybe I should have, but I just wasn't as bright as my twin sister, and I had to be told several times before I got it. It wasn't that I wanted to be trouble for him. I just wasn't as mature or insightful as my sister. I became scared to do anything for fear of whipping or being responsible for replacing a piece of furniture or a refrigerator full of food.

Even now, I wonder why bouncing down the stairs bothered him so. The staircase had a wall on one side and two rails on the open side, so there was no way we could fall off the stairs. Bouncing from step to step wouldn't allow us to fall forward down the stairs. Not once did any of us ever fall down those stairs. I guess he just didn't like our laughter. Our giggling always annoyed him. Even though my sister was just as guilty, even more so because it was her idea, I was punished, and she wasn't even spoken to. Sometimes I would say it was her idea, but he didn't care. He wouldn't punish her. If two children are guilty of doing the same thing, why is only one punished? And why was bouncing down the stairs considered bad behavior?

In my opinion, misbehavior is doing what you were told not to do or not doing what you were told to do. Most of the things I got a whipping for were not things I had been told not to do or things that I was told to do and didn't do. However, there were two things that I had been told to do on a regular basis and that I failed at many times. One was to make my bed. I never intended to not make my bed. I didn't wake up and decide, "I'm not making my bed today." I was in a hurry to go to the bathroom or down to breakfast or out to play and never got around to it. That was the burr under my father's saddle. He would not tolerate an unmade bed. Leaving a bed unmade proved the person was of low character, careless, had no self-respect, and would not become a responsible adult. He would go upstairs and check every day. Anytime he discovered my bed unmade, rather than tell me to go make it, he would whip me. If my mother knew I had not made my bed, she would, in her gentle voice, tell me to go make my bed. I would. Why couldn't my father act that way?

My father's whippings were five and six hard hits to my bottom along with a scolding. I also would slam the screened door. Not on purpose. I was just in a hurry. As usual, a whipping would occur. If my father was working, and I slammed the door again, my mother would gently say, "Don't slam the door." I just didn't catch on like my twin sister. Ever. But it wasn't my fault that I wasn't as smart as she was. *Is.* Kids mature differently and at different speeds. Being fraternal twins means you are different and sometimes very different.

From my earliest days, I was shy. I would hide behind my mother or my twin sister when meeting new people. I felt safe behind my mother. My mother was never too busy to hug or kiss us, stroke our hair, or wipe away tears. But when my father scolded me or threatened a whipping, she stayed quiet. After the punishment, I would hurry to my mother, and she would console me and tell me it would be all right. She would hug me and love on me until I was satisfied that she still loved me. Her touch was soft and gentle, like her way of speaking. She was so opposite to my father.

When my father felt a whipping was due me, my older sister would go to my mother, and my twin would stay close to me, watching with wide, sad eyes and a look of apprehension on her face. I can still see that look. Then as usual, she would say, "Let's go upstairs, My," or "Let's go outside and play, My." All my offenses were treated the same. There was never a degree of difference in my punishment for the different wrongdoings. Slamming the screen door, laughing too loud (he hated that), talking too loud (another of his hates), talking too much, not making my bed (which was a felony), running through the house, having to be called inside at dusk, again—each offense was punishable with a whipping. I'm not talking about a spanking. I'm talking about a whipping. Most everything I was guilty of, my sister was also guilty of (except making her bed), but his focus was always on me. This fact was not completely lost on me.

My father hated it when I got excited over something. Going for ice cream or on a picnic was something exciting for me. And I would burst out with laughter and excitement, and he would command, "Calm down! Don't be so loud! What's the matter with you?" He often asked me that question, all through my years under his roof. I never knew how to answer him. I never answered him when I was young because I didn't know what the matter with me was. When I was older, in my teens, I was afraid to answer the question because I feared he would consider it sassing. He would give me a long, stern expression. I would crumble. The mood to go wherever we had plans to go to plunged. I feared getting excited and running and laughing with my sister would bring on a whipping, so I tried to tamper down my enthusiasm.

I was not always successful. He frequently dampened my spirits. He expected his children—five years old, twelve years old, and sixteen years old—to never get excited…always be adults in their behavior.

Starting School

STARTING SCHOOL WAS both exciting and frightening for me. When we started school, my twin sister and I were placed in the same class. Our teacher was Mrs. Allman. I liked her because I believed she really liked me. Every day, between subjects we studied, we'd have breaks to get a drink of water from the water fountain between the boys' and the girls' restrooms. Each class had its own restrooms in the back of the classroom near where we hung our coats and sweaters. I followed my sister and stood by the door waiting my turn. I asked my sister to wait for me, and she agreed. However, when I came out of the restroom, my sister wasn't waiting for me. I cried. I asked her why she didn't wait for me, and she told me the teacher told her to come take her seat. I dried my tears then because I realized my best friend had not abandoned me. Even in the first grade, I so very much depended on my sister, who was my very best friend.

Well into the school year, Mrs. Allman invited parents to come visit the classroom. As usual, Mrs. Allman had the student, in our case students, sit with the mother in a semicircle directly in front of the chalkboard (*blackboard* back then). She wrote a word on the blackboard and asked my sister if she could read it. My sister thought and then felt like she wasn't sure. So I raised my hand, and Mrs. Allman asked me to read it. I did! The word was *work*. And I was proud that I knew it when my smart sister didn't. But I also was sorry that I knew it and she didn't. It was already well established, at least in our home, that I lacked the mental capacity of my sister.

Mrs. Allman told my mother that I had artistic talent. She showed my mother a hand that I had drawn and compared it to the other students' drawings. She said, "It looks like a real hand." I was a little proud and surprised that I was being noted for doing something well. It made me feel important and confident that I could do something well and that I wasn't a total failure.

Our school was built like an H. The part connecting the two sides was where the offices, lunchroom, and gym were. The gym is also where we had school functions like Christmas programs and plays. On one occasion, my twin sister stepped too close to the edge of the stage and fell off. My father ran to her and picked her up. I wondered if it had been me if my father would have whipped me right then and there. (Several years later at my grandparents' home, I stepped on a shard of glass, and my father scolded me.) Now that we were in school, I felt like I was as smart as anyone, except my twin sister, or I wouldn't have been allowed to go to school. I hoped that I would not fail at any of the work required of me so my father wouldn't criticize me or whip me. I had hoped that he would realize that I wasn't completely unable to learn.

When I learned that my twin sister and I would not be together in second grade, I cried. I really needed her. I so depended on her in many ways. She was my strength. She was my helper. She was my best friend. I knew she loved me without condition. And when I needed her, she was always there for me, even at my whippings and after them. Second grade was challenging for me. I didn't have my twin sister, my best friend, my confidant with me. I did have a gentle, patient teacher, much to my relief. I saw my sister at recess and at lunch break, and we walked home together. At this time in my life, I did not fear going home.

My mother would greet us, love on us, ask about our day at school, and send us to our rooms to change clothes to go outside to play. On warm days, my twin sister and I played outside a good deal of the time. For now, I wasn't frightened to be inside when my father returned, but I did wonder how things would go.

I liked school. I liked my teacher. I believed, unlike my father, that I was capable of learning. I felt a certain amount of freedom at school. I wasn't judged or threatened. I was very, very shy. It wasn't easy making friends. What if they didn't like me? But I so looked forward to meeting up with my twin sister at recess and at lunch and to go home.

As the years went by, my dread and fear of going to school multiplied. By fifth grade, I was afraid of asking questions. Everyone would know I was dumb. I was afraid of answering questions. What if I give the wrong answer? I avoided the teacher's glance. I never raised my hand. I became extremely nervous and fearful in class. Fear of the unknown was always before me. What if?

My father's judging of my mental capabilities increased. His presumptions that I would fail increased. His negative descriptions of me increased. I began to grow in fear and dread of another day.

I no longer liked school.

The Paddle

OFTEN, AS MY twin sister and I were playing outside, my father would call to me to come inside. I would wonder what I had done. I had to have done something; otherwise, he also would have called for my sister to come inside. Almost always, a scenario like that proved me right. I had a whipping coming. Rather than correcting me and seeing the issue through this child's eyes, he judged me guilty and sentenced me to a whipping. My mother would stand idly by. Most of the "misbehavior" I was guilty of was not in disobedience to him. They weren't the result of doing something that I was told not to do, or vice versa. They were things that agitated him, grated on him. It was as though he couldn't understand child behavior or child thinking. But children aren't born with an adult mindset.

But also as usual, my mother was there to console me, wipe away the tears, and quietly send me on my way. Feeling refreshed and loved, I would return to play with my sister. Sometimes in situations like this throughout our years as young children, my sister would ask if I got a whipping. When I admitted to it, she would say, "I'm sorry, My."

Sometimes she asked me why I got a whipping and what had I done. I would reply, "I don't know." When my sister and I were doing the same things, I wondered why I received a whipping and she didn't. It was not unusual for my father to watch my sister and me as we played outside. I think he was watching to see if I did something that he disapproved of so he could get on me.

The things for which I was punished were not bad or wrong but things that children do because they are still children. Things he seemed to not understand as childhood attitudes and frame of mind. He saw my infractions as misbehavior rather than the perspective of a child. Everything was considered misbehavior, intentional disobedience. Nothing was ever considered an accident. I never in my life intentionally disobeyed my parents. I didn't want to dishonor my mother. I was afraid of my father. And I knew Jesus was watching. When I would explain that it was my sister's idea, my father would say, "I don't care." Then the whipping would come.

By the time I was seven years old, I knew my father didn't like me. I just wasn't sure why. It could have been because I wasn't as smart as my twin sister. It could have been because I was a bad person. It could have been because I wasn't good or successful at anything. It could have been because I laughed a lot with my sister. It could have been that I talked or laughed too loudly or too much. When my sister and I were playing on the living room floor, and we were laughing loudly and often, he would peek from behind his newspaper and glare at me. As always, I melted. My mother sat quietly by. There was just something about me that so displeased him, that so peeved him. My naturalness was such an issue with him.

It was the year when I would turn eight that my father made a wooden paddle to use to whip me. It was summertime. (I guess from all the whippings he gave me and for future whippings, he thought it wise to have something harder than his hand.) It was solid wood, about six inches by four inches, about a half an inch thick with a handle long enough for his hand to grasp comfortably.

One day I was in the kitchen with my mother when she went to the utility closet and took it down from the nail where it hung and showed it to me. She said, "Your daddy made this for you," in a gentle way. I was stunned. I stood there speechless, not knowing what to say. As she rehung it, I walked away. Even now, after almost a lifetime, I wonder why she showed it to me. She spoke it so matter-of-factly. She didn't look disturbed or worried or sad. Just normal. Like she was showing me a new platter or pitcher. How did she expect me to respond? I remember that moment so well; we were in the kitchen, the window was behind me, the sink to my left, my mother standing directly in front of me by the utility closet. Why was she showing it to me? Was it a warning? She was so calm. What was going through her mind right then? Confusion and fear were going through mine.

My mother allowed my father to be the total disciplinarian. She interfered only twice. One day, my father was furious with me for something that I did not do. I think I was eight or nine. One of my sisters did whatever I was about to be punished for. He would not listen to my pleas of innocence. My family gathered in the living room in a haphazard circle, anticipating my whipping. My father had hold of my left wrist, as usual. To my right stood my twin sister, next to her was my mother. My father was scolding me for something that I couldn't recall, and my mother told him, "You're not whipping this child." I don't know why she protested this whipping, why it was any different from the others.

He replied to her, "You stay out of this or I'll whip you next."

I remember standing there, shaking with fear, my heart pounding. She backed down. Her backing down broke my heart because she wasn't willing to be hurt in my place. She wasn't willing to suffer for me. She would rather I be the one to be whipped. Two heartbreaks in one minute. This time I received a brutal flogging. My father was unhinged. He was out of control, whipping me wildly, all around the living room floor. I wrestled my hand loose, but I couldn't escape the hitting because he latched onto the other wrist. My mother and both sisters begged him to stop, but he continued until he was exhausted. It was summertime; I remember because the oscillating fan was rotating on a table. Many years later, as a young adult, I showed a scar on my left hand, the outside part near my wrist, to my twin sister. I told her I didn't know how I got it. She said, "That's one time when Daddy whipped you so hard, and your hand hit the fan. Blood squirted everywhere." I don't remember anything after my father ended his thrashing.

Not only did my father not like me; there was nothing about me that he approved of. He never praised me, encouraged me, or bragged on me as he did my twin sister. The only time he spoke to me was to scold me, accuse me of some kind of disobedience, or tell me to do something. But he did two things for me that I considered a blessing. When I was around ten years old, he bought my twin sister and me each a Hula-Hoop. Hers was blue; mine was green. The other thing was he brought a stack of unprinted newspapers home from where he worked, for me to draw on. (I loved to draw.) Both times I was so excited, and surprised. He almost appeared happy in the giving.

Another time I must have done something really bad because I got another really hard whipping. I was eight or nine years old. It seems like between ages seven and twelve, I angered and disappointed my father so many times because he whipped me often and hard. There was something about me that he just could not tolerate or endure. My father had more control of the whipping and himself. He wasn't crazy with wrath like he was the other time he whipped me furiously. He was almost methodical with each slap of the wooden paddle. This time he hit my bottom extremely hard, over and over, eight or nine times, with complete control of the situation, confident with each slap of that wooden paddle. Those slaps to my backside left welts that hurt so badly that I couldn't sit down or walk. I went to bed. A little later my mother came to me to put salve on my wounds. She said to me, "If you would be a good little girl, your daddy wouldn't spank you." There, she said it. I was not a good little girl. I was bad. Bad to the core. And I didn't know what to do to change and become a good little girl. I was just being me. None of the things I did were bad. I truly was a good little girl. I just did things that irked my father. Things that aggravated him, got on his last nerve. But what I did was not disobedience. I *never* intentionally disobeyed my father. I was afraid to. To this day, I have no idea what I did to deserve that whipping. Not only did it leave sores on my bottom, it broke my heart. This whipping proved to me that my father really did want to hurt me. I was learning that he just plain did not like me at all.

When I was nine or ten, we went to my maternal grandparents' home for Christmas. When I heard that my uncle's family was arriving with their three sons, just a few years older than we were, from out of state, my sisters and I were so excited. We hadn't seen them in several years. I was bouncing around and laughing, all excited, when my father commanded me to "Stop that, and get quiet and sit down! And don't you get up until I say so!" I glanced at my mother. No reaction. I was crushed. And embarrassed. I caught my grandfather's gaze. I wondered if he was judging me or pitying me. I still remember the look on his face—not really expressing his emotions. (My mother looked so much like my grandfather.)

Does the Punishment Fit the Crime?

SOME PEOPLE, SUCH as my father, believe that a parent needs to show the child that he is bigger, stronger, more powerful, and more determined than the child is. The parent, usually the father, wants to prove that he's boss and that what he says goes. No questions asked. No debate. These parents want to completely control the child, even what's innate in the child, and what's inherent in the child. I believe that my father was trying to break me, to break my spirit. It was like there was something about me, something *inside* me that he was trying to beat out of me. He was trying to undo me and make me the way he wanted me to be inside and outside. I felt like he was punishing me for being me, who I was, what I was. There was not one redeeming quality about me to my father. I was just a bother and a burden, and bad, the three B's. And a waste of his time and energy. I realized by age ten that I did not like my father.

They say a parent should reassure the child after the punishment, that they should let the child know he is still loved and accepted. After my punishment, my father criticized me again and told me to "Go on!" In other words, "Leave me. Go off somewhere out of my sight."

I read somewhere a preacher's take on punishment. Paraphrased, he said that when a parent beats a child, they are imposing themselves on the child. (To *impose* means to force or inflict something on someone; to lay on a burden;

to bring about by force or authority; to force one's self on or take advantage of someone; and to demand, enforce, inflict, exact, require, coerce, penalize). That cancels out the individuality of the child. Beating the child tells him that he is a bad person—not that he behaved badly and that he needs to be *punished* as opposed to being *corrected*. A child who is beaten doesn't become strong. In all reality, he becomes weak and angry. Punishment makes the child feel guilt and shame about what he has done to be beaten. (You don't learn from guilt or shame.) Punishment is meant to make the child *suffer* for breaking the rules. It's getting back at the child as a form of *revenge*.

My opinion of *punishment* in the form of beatings is this: It makes the child feel resentful, intimidated, fearful of authority figures, fearful of being judged, fearful of being rejected, feeling inferior, unworthy, hopeless, and unaccepted as they are, and that he is a bad person, not that he did wrong or did a bad thing. Not that he does wrong but that he is wrong, inside. Their innateness is wrong, a mistake. Unlikable. Beating the child will destroy their selfness, their individuality, their uniqueness that God put in them, which sets them apart from everyone else. It will strip them of their true identity. It also can and will stifle the call God has put on their life. Punishments like beatings turn the child's heart away from the parent. It drives a wedge between parent and child. Punishment is personal; it's an attack on the person of the child. Punishment is not teaching.

Discipline in the form of correction focuses on correcting bad behavior. It defines the wrong and explains why it's wrong. It allows the child the opportunity and the time to absorb the facts about doing the thing that has been labeled wrong. It's training the child to understand why this particular act was wrong and unacceptable. Discipline should teach the child good behavior, not punish for the bad.

Parents and those in authority need to realize that children aren't born with the capacity to understand as adults do. God doesn't punish His children, so why do we punish ours? He corrects His children because we learn through correction. Punishment destroys; correction encourages.

When I was parenting my young son and saw things he did that I got whippings for, I told him not to do whatever because…and I gave him the reason why. When he repeated the wrong, I didn't lose my temper because I realized he was a child, and he didn't think the way I did. He didn't have the perspective that I did. Kids don't always remember to do or not to do things regularly. It is a learning process. Children need time, years, to acclimate to adult thinking, to adjust their ability to understand reasons for specific behavior. Children aren't born with life experiences. And children are different from other children, even with siblings.

My father wanted my sisters and me to be just alike. But God made each of us uniquely. Children mature at different speeds. I believe that God puts in us characteristics for a reason, for a purpose. I'm not referring to our calling; I'm speaking about our individuality, our personalities, likes, dislikes, quirks, tastes, and inclinations. We each have a specialty about us, that thing that God puts in us that drives us and motivates us, even inadvertently, unknowingly to us as children, that makes us distinct. Punishment, especially done in anger, distorts self-confidence. It twists the inner self, the innateness, and the oneness of the child. Harsh punishment is personal. God doesn't use a cookie cutter to create His children. He uses a pattern for a child then discards it and makes another pattern for the next child. Nor does He beat us when we misbehave or do wrong or do something in the gray area (the gray area being something that annoys or irritates the parent but isn't *wrong* in and of itself).

After I was branded "a bad little girl," I felt rather hopeless. I didn't know how to be a "good little girl." The things for which I was whipped weren't bad. They were just annoyances, irritants. Even mistakes like knocking over something or being too loud. When I did these things while my father was at work, my mother never reacted. She never punished me. From this whipping on, I tried to stay out of my father's way. I wouldn't look at him because I knew he wanted to catch my eye and then start prodding me. (As I aged, his prodding me, his nudging me to get mad at him and react, increased.) However, every night I kissed him as I was going to bed.

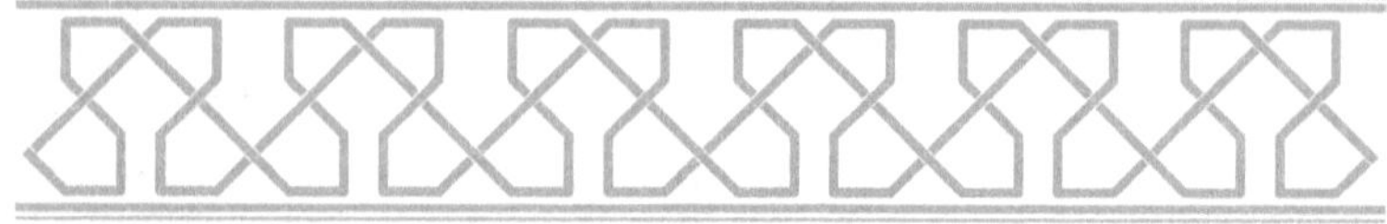

Under Conviction of Another Father I Feared

When we were eight years old, my twin sister and I came under the conviction of God. She decided to get saved and then was baptized. Therefore, my parents decided that I, too, should get saved. I, on the other hand, didn't want another father. The one I had was more than enough. I had been taught that God was a Father whom we should obey, but if I couldn't obey the one I had, how could I obey the one who lived in heaven? He was even bigger and more powerful than the one I already had. On top of that, I didn't believe that God loved me. I believed He just wanted to conquer me and control me. I felt like He was a bigger version of my earthly father. And that to me was scary. Also, I wondered how He could love someone like me, who was a bad girl. I also believed that the only reason I was included in the "whosoever will" was because the Bible was written before I was born, and God couldn't change what He said. So I ran.

My mother's father was a pastor of a church in the same denomination as the church where we went. I was very proud of him. My mother taught adult women's Bible study for many, many years. My father taught preteen boys for several years and was a deacon. I'm sure he was thought to be honorable and righteous on the outside. We were in church Sunday mornings, Sunday nights, Wednesday nights, for GAs, and later on, in our teens, youth group, and youth choir. But my father insisted that I was bad, rebellious, disrespectful, disobedient (intentionally), and on my way to prison. Every Saturday night, my mother would gather the three of us together to study our Sunday school lesson recorded in our Sunday school quarterly booklet. We did our Bible readings according to our booklet before we got into our beds. One night as I climbed into bed, I remembered that I hadn't read the scriptures. I didn't want to get out of bed to read, so I decided not to. Then I heard a voice say, "Why do this to Me?" I knew it was Jesus.

I thought, *Because You let my daddy hurt me.*

But I got out of bed and read. And continued reading night after night after night.

Every day I would pray in the morning before we went to school that I would do well and that my teacher would not call on me. I knew that I would not know the answer to her question or the math problem. I prayed this prayer every day all through school. It didn't always work.

One day, a Saturday, at the age of ten, I was playing with my sister in our room when my father called my name. (He seldom called me by my name. He almost always used my nickname, My.) Fear struck my heart like lightning strikes a building. I wondered what I had done and suspected that I was going to get a whipping. I stopped playing and got up quickly for fear—again there's that word *fear*—that I was in trouble. But I descended the stairs slowly, holding on to every second it took to get to the first floor. When I turned to enter the living room, I saw my mother sitting on the sofa. I wondered what on earth I had done. It must have been bad because my mother was there waiting for me, and she never was all the other times that I was in trouble. I hesitated. My father said, in his natural matter-of-fact voice, "Come sit beside your mother." I did so, then he sat on my other side.

He began the conversation. He and my mother believed that I was under conviction and that I needed to be saved.

I knew about salvation. I read my little white Bible every night. I attended Sunday School every week where I heard about God and His love. But I wasn't sure that God had a personal love for me. Actually, I was afraid of Him. I saw Him as a big version of my father and that He had the same opinion of me as my earthly father did, and if I accepted Him as my heavenly Father, how would He treat me? I feared His punishment and judgment and scorn. John 3:16 says,

> For God so loved the world that He gave His only begotten Son that whosoever believes in Him shall not perish but have eternal life.

Really? Even me? There are exceptions to every rule, aren't there? Maybe I was the exception. I mean, God has His standards to maintain. Why would He include me? Why would He call a bad, defective, wrong person like me? Why would He want someone who *was* wrong, not just did wrong? There is a difference. I had memorized many scriptures, but sometimes they were just words, or words meant for other people, people who did wrong but weren't wrong. Believing He really did intentionally include me was a stretch. He wrote John 3:16 years ago and couldn't remove it from the Bible now, so He had to honor it. So I believed salvation was offered to me on a technicality.

I wanted Him to love me the way His Word described His love, but it was difficult to believe because, after all, He didn't stop my father from hurting me, right? I knew that my parents were right about my being under conviction. I felt God's conviction daily, hourly. I sat there having mixed emotions. They each spoke about salvation and heaven. I fully understood salvation and sin. I was a very proficient, prolific sinner, so I knew about sin. And I felt conviction heavy on my heart. I believed that God was determined to turn me around the way my father did, not with physical beatings but verbally. I believed He was convicting me in a judgmental manner. But I knew I needed saving—maybe salvation would turn me into a good person. So I decided to accept Jesus into my heart and said the sinner's prayer.

That was November 15, 1958. The next day, Sunday, I walked down that short but what appeared to be a very long aisle to where the pastor stood and made my decision public. The song that we sang during the invitation to be saved was "Just as I Am." My thoughts on that song were that "Just as I Am" referred to my characteristics, not my misbehavior or sins. I knew that I never intentionally went against my father's standards, but like everyone else, I did commit sin. However, this song alluded to all the negative points of my being that my father declared about me. It inferred that my worthlessness and inferiority, lack of mental acuity, and so on did not prevent me from being saved. God accepted and loved me despite my poor character. I still remember what I wore that Sunday. I wore a yellow, ruffled, dotted Swiss short-sleeved blouse with a navy calico skirt and black patent leather buckle shoes, with white dress socks.

I didn't completely trust God. My father taught me, in the way he treated me and in the way he talked to me, that I wasn't valued, that I wasn't loved. That I wasn't deserving of any mercy or kindness or favor. If God was anything like my earthly father, I was in big trouble. But if He truly forgives sin, I knew I needed Him in my life, and I would keep Him busy. I reasoned that if He would forgive me of all my wickedness, He couldn't be all bad.

After my salvation experience, life for me intensified. My father was even harder on me. He must have expected me to become a saint overnight. That didn't happen. My decision to follow Jesus was real. I was determined to follow Him, even if He never liked me.

I'm sure my father expected my salvation to be the miracle that I needed to turn me into a saint or an ideal adult-like child who would make me smart, cancel out all my mistakes and failures, and set me on the road to perfection. Apparently, he was sorely disillusioned. As time went on, my punishments were not for my misbehavior or disobedience or irritants or annoyances but rather for my disappointments to my father. He was always disgruntled with me, always frustrated with me, always discontented with me. He was always in a negative attitude toward me. He wouldn't talk with me. He talked *to* me, always matter-of-factly or angrily. There was never any patience, or tenderness, or understanding, only critical comments or remarks. I guess I expected a miracle too. I thought God would turn me into a good person who did well, was smart and lovable, and never made mistakes. So we both were disappointed. I was still the defective one, mentally challenged, intentionally bad, beyond hope, and of course, very different than my twin sister who was smart and never made mistakes and who was always successful at everything she attempted. Individuality, being different, as a pair of fraternal twins are, was just not right. What made my twin sister *her* and what made me *me* were fairly different, and my father was just not happy about it. To him, my inborn features, the traits I was born with, were wrong. And he was determined to change them.

Gradually, I became fearful of all kinds of things. Not necessarily of natural things to fear but illogical things. There wasn't a defining moment or event that woke me to the realization. It slowly sneaked up on me. I was afraid of my teachers because they soon would learn how dumb I was. I was afraid of anyone in authority because they had the power to punish me. I was afraid of meeting new people because they wouldn't like me. (My father told me many times that I would never have any friends because when they got to know me, they would find out what kind of person I really was.) I was fearful of asking questions out loud because people would find out how dumb I was. I was fearful of being asked a question because I probably wouldn't know the answer— what if I was wrong? I was afraid of taking tests because I knew that I would fail. I was fearful of people looking at me or watching me because I suspected they were judging me and finding some kind of fault in me. I was afraid of asking for help because that would prove me inept, incompetent, or helpless. I became cautious of trying new things, like games and sports, because I knew I would fail. When fear came over me, I would cry. I cried a lot.

In sixth grade, I began self-deprecating. I called myself ugly, critical names. I would ask myself why I couldn't do anything right, why I was a failure. I was ashamed of being dumb and wondered why God didn't make me smart like my sister. My hope of doing well at things began to flounder. Where I had been a spontaneous, bubbly child, I became an introvert and self-reflective. I began to judge myself harshly. Since I was continually compared to my twin sister, I even felt like my personal opinions and likes were wrong. I tried to change my attitudes about likes and dislikes, but that didn't work. Deep down, I still liked what I liked and disliked what I disliked. I would begin to cry in difficult situations or if I was put on the spot. Fear of the unknown became paramount. I carried around with me an enormous weight of impending gloom.

The week my twin sister and I turned twelve years old, we went to church camp. It was our first year to go. I loved going to camp. There I had the freedom to be me. No one watching me, waiting for me to mess up. No one there judged me or criticized me or threatened to whip me. There was no one to tell me that I was without hope or that there was something wrong with me or that I was a bad person. The counselors and staff treated me the same way they treated the other girls.

Besides having Bible study, doing crafts, having quiet time and free time, we had chapel service on Friday night. Every year they had a different missionary from a foreign country to share his story. This year the missionary was from Africa, East Africa, a country called Tanganyika. (The following year, Tanganyika consolidated with the island, Zanzibar, just off the coast, and then changed their name to Tanzania.) The missionary was named Thomas Tipton, his wife was Virginia, and they had a four-year-old son, they called Tommy.

Bro. Tipton described their life in Tanganyika. He talked about the people, their homes, and his work. He told of humorous events that had everyone laughing. He shared stories that touched us. I could have sat there for hours, mes-merized, hanging onto every word. I fell in love with Africa. I wanted to go to Africa. I wanted to be a missionary to Africa. Africa had grabbed my heart and wouldn't let go. (As I write this, I am brought to tears. My love for Africa is still strong.) He taught us a phrase in Swahili that I could repeat for two decades, but then because I stopped repeating it, I forgot it. The last thing Bro. Tipton said to us was, "I hope someday I can look out across the river and see some of you coming across in a boat to help me."

My heart pounded, hard. My emotions almost got the best of me. I wanted to run down that aisle and take Bro. Tipton's hand and say, "God called *me*, an inferior, hopeless, bad-to-the-core twelve-year-old to be a missionary to Africa!" But I didn't. I knew that I knew that God had called me to go to Africa as a missionary. But I also knew that I wasn't smart enough. I would never be smart enough to be a missionary anywhere. And I was a bad person who didn't know how to not be bad. My father had instilled in me that I had mental difficulties, and I knew that would prevent me from being able to learn what I needed to learn to go anywhere and be a missionary. I left the little tabernacle joyful and sad. That week had been the best week of my young life. The next day we went home. I dreaded it. I didn't tell anyone about my calling until 1988 when I told my two best friends.

I wanted to tell my mother, but I believed if I told her, she would be so proud of me and so happy that she would want my father to know, maybe believing he would accept me. I felt like my father would not believe that God would call me, that I was being foolish. Or it was wishful thinking. That would be a way of taking it away from me. I believed that he would say, "You? Why would God call you to be a missionary? He wants good people, people who are smart, respectful, and obedient. You just need to forget about that." I didn't tell my twin sister because I knew that she would tell our mother.

In the nineties, one day when my mother was ill (she had been a widow for a few years), I sent her a get-well card, and in it, I told her about my call to Africa. About two weeks later, she was hospitalized. I went to stay with her for a few days. I was nervous. I finally asked her if she got my card and what she thought about my note. She began to weep and said, "God understands." I don't know if she wept because I didn't have the self-confidence to fulfill the call, or if it was because she felt blessed that I received the call. Or maybe she felt bad that my father was responsible for my lack of self-confidence. It was never mentioned again. Nevertheless, I *loved* Africa. I held her deeply in my heart. My calling was precious to me. I felt special, accepted, valued, and worthy. I cherished it like it was a treasure from someone special. I thought about it, dreamed about it, loved it. Wept over it. And deep down I hoped. Oddly enough, in the 1980s, while we were still sharing Christmas with my mother's sister's family, her daughter made collages for me and my sisters. Not so surprisingly, mine was of Africa. She had no idea. I laughed and wept.

Sticks and Stones…and Words

BELIEVING THE NEGATIVE words my father spoke over me began slowly. When I was young, something inside me refused to believe them. But they did hurt. However, day after day, month after month, year after year, they took their toll. By the time I reached my teens, I began to agree with him. His words still hurt me, but I knew he was right.

When I entered the eighth grade, my mother started working outside the home. I so dreaded it. I was always afraid to come home when my father was on the day shift because he would get home right after we got home from school. I presumed that somehow I would get in trouble. It didn't take much for me to provoke my father. Any infraction caused him to become angry toward me. When school let out at three o'clock, a dread would descend on me. My pleasant, humorous attitude became gloomy and frightened. My father got home around half-past four. For an hour, I was comfortable and relaxed and enjoyed being at home with my sisters. When the door opened, and my father stepped into the house, a light-switch effect occurred inside me. I became a different person. With my two sisters, I felt safe and accepted, like one of them. But my father's arrival changed that, daily.

I did well in school until the fifth grade. I guess that's when my father's criticism took hold of my attitude. I believed that I was incapable of learning, so why try? I would just prove to my father that I was a failure. In the seventh grade, I was average. I did very well in a couple of subjects from then on, but I struggled in a couple. It was like my father's treatment of me and his feelings about me paralyzed my learning ability. My mental capability seemed to shut down. I began to suffer from depression and real sadness.

My father's discipline of me became less about my behavior (I guess because I had grown up a little these last couple of years) and more about my person. By age fourteen, when the mood hit him or after a period of time where there had been no reason to get on me, his temper would flare up, and he would start in on me. I listened but tried not to respond. Sometimes he would make a remark that insinuated that I was lazy and didn't care about anything because I wasn't doing anything constructive. "Can't you find something to do besides sitting there with a magazine (or a book or a sketch pad)?"

I would reply, very calmly, and sincerely, "What do you want me to do?"

Then he would say, "Anything. Just get busy!" I would leave the room and go to the kitchen or up to my room. I figured he just didn't want me around. The feeling was mutual.

At age fourteen, I still received physical whippings. They occurred on average once a week, sometimes twice, not because of any disobedience but because I needed one. Several days a week, my father would criticize me even with just one remark. It was about me rather than my misbehavior. How much disobedience could a teen girl be guilty of who was very conscious of her relationship with Jesus, who only went to church (several times a week), and school? I never smoked, I never drank, I never took drugs, I never cussed, I never sassed, and I never left the house without permission. I asked permission for everything that I wanted or wanted to do.

As I entered my teenage years and had matured some, I began to notice the glare from my father's eyes that he would give me just before a whipping would occur or before a scolding started. The glare itself was frightening. It was a warning of something to come. He continually berated me and belittled me. I was absolutely of no earthly value to him. I knew that I was a burden in several ways. In later years, I wondered what he would have been like had I not been born.

My father's expectations of my twin sister were much less demanding. He favored her, I think, because of her ability and desire to learn. My attitude was, "Why bother?" I didn't have the brains to learn, so my attempt at learning was futile, useless, and a waste of time and effort. I studied just to get promoted in school. As in elementary school, in high school, I was fearful of people finding out how dumb I was. I never raised my hand to answer a question in class. I feared the teacher would call on me for something, and I would fail at whatever it was, answering a question, a math problem, whatever.

Every day I would ask God to not let my teacher call on me. My father constantly compared me to my sister, constantly reminding me how smart she was. Sometimes he would ask, "Why can't you be like her?" He also reminded me that she was respectful, obedient, and a good person. But around the age of fifteen, my sister started standing up to him. She would tell him that he was too strict, that he allowed us little freedom, and that he didn't trust us to make our own decisions. He would listen and tell her that we were still kids and needed to be controlled. He never responded in anger. She never got in trouble with her accusations. He always listened and then explained his reason for such control and then walked away. He treated us so differently. For years, he wondered why I couldn't be like my twin sister. In a few more years, he would tell me that I would never be like her.

My father continued to instill in me that I was defective, that there was something wrong with me, and that I was incapable of learning and reasoning and would require help in my daily living as an adult. Sometimes in a low-key, serious voice, he would say, "You're not right," "You won't be able to make it on your own," or "You might as well accept that you're not like other people." Sometimes he would say these things when no one was around, sometimes in front of our family. (My mother would remain quiet.) Tears would well up in my eyes and then run down my cheeks, and then I would break down and sob. He would turn and walk away. A part of me disagreed with his assumptions, but in time, I gradually began to believe his words of negativity and discouragement. In a few years, I would be completely in agreement with my father's opinion of me. I was not smart enough to think for myself and not a whole person.

As a child, my father watched me like a hawk eyeing a chicken or a rodent. I think he expected me to misbehave, make a mistake, or initiate an accident. Maybe hoping I would mess up. He seemed to enjoy his power over me. Even when I did something accidentally, like spill something or knock something over, he would fuss at me and criticize me. As a teen, he knew my days of misbehavior and disobedience were basically over, but my character was still an issue. Obviously, I had not changed inside for the better. Maybe my flaws were worsening.

The tongue can wield great power. The Bible says in Proverbs 18:21 (CSB),

> Death and life are in the power of the
> tongue and those who love it will eat its
> fruit.

Some Bible commentaries say those who speak the words will eat their fruit. If you speak criticism and negativity, the words will condemn you. Some commentaries say which words you believe or accept are the fruit you eat. Either way, we must be careful what words we use when we speak.

> But what comes out of the mouth comes
> from the heart. (Matthew 15:18 GNT)

Our words tell what's in our hearts. My father had a lot of anger and resentment toward me in his heart. Words can encourage and bless, or they can discourage and tear down.

> Every way of a man seems right in his
> own eyes, but the Lord weighs the heart.
> (Proverbs 12:2 NKJV)

What's our motive? What's our purpose? Do we intend to build up or tear down? "Sticks and stones may break my bones, but words will never harm me" is a lie. Words hurt worse than physical hurts. And they last a lot longer. Sometimes forever. They cut to the very core of a person. They are intentional and purposeful, powerful, and personal. They confuse, teach, torment, and leave lasting scars.

My father was very negative, very pessimistic. He saw only the bad that possibly could occur. "If you play in the street, you will get run over. Don't get back on the horse because you will fall off again. Don't keep trying because you will keep failing. Keep the storm door locked because someone will come in and hurt you." These weren't a possibility but an assurance of what would happen.

During my mid-teens, my father's discipline started with a negative remark about me as a person. Sometimes it caught me by surprise. I would be minding my own business, quietly. He would, out of the blue, make a critical comment and look at me. I did not respond as I returned a look. Then he would push the issue. It wasn't about something that I was doing that was wrong but rather an irritant. I wasn't doing anything important. Sometimes I would ask, "What?" He would start speaking negative words over me, how bad I was and how I would not amount to anything. I was a failure and always would be. Soon he would work up enough anger to tell me to get to the kitchen. I knew a whipping was coming, but often I didn't know why. The most that I would say when a whipping was threatened, was to ask what I had done to get a whipping. I remember times that I would ask, "What did I do? What did I do?"

My father would either tell me, "Be quiet. Don't sass me," or he would say, "You know what you did," or sometimes he would tell me, "You need to be taught a lesson." When he told me to do something, I did it. When he told me not to do something, I didn't. When he told me to do it over, "the right way," I would. I was obedient and cautious around him. Sometimes when he was belittling me, I wouldn't speak (but I would cry), and he would ask, "Do you hear me? Answer me!" I never knew how to respond to him. I began believing that my father hated something deep inside me, and his whippings were trying to beat it out of me.

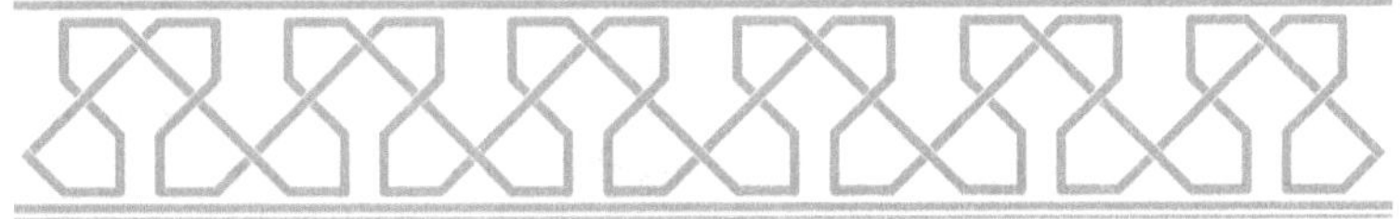

More Rejection

WHEN WE WERE fourteen, my twin sister started hanging around my older sister. They became close friends. I wonder if they began to get close when my father would start on me and the two of them would go to my older sister's room and close the door. I guess they felt safe in there.

When my older sister started her sophomore year at high school, my twin sister and I were still going to junior high at age fourteen. It was grades seven through nine. Perhaps because of their time hiding in my older sister's bedroom, they became close. They would go into her room, close the door, and exclude me. I wondered why I was always banned, excluded. But then, why not? They would do homework at the kitchen table. I would hear them laughing and talking about boys and clothes the other girls were wearing, which teacher was liked, and which teacher was strict. I was always on the couch, alone. Sometimes I would gather my books and homework papers and go to the kitchen and join them. Suddenly they would get quiet. I waited. Sometimes I would ask why they stopped talking, but neither would answer. I would gather my things and return to the living room. Then I would hear them laughing and talking again, and I would sob. This was a very lonely time for me. Even my sisters didn't care about me. This scenario would repeat itself until my older sister graduated and went to college.

My father would criticize me and mock me for not being as smart as my twin sister. He would make a remark about my lack of intelligence and then become angry because I wasn't as smart as my sister was. Then it would evolve into my poor character, and then I would be whipped for those limitations. If I couldn't help being short-brained, why punish me for it? Through my mid- to upper teens, he would make negative comments about me or to me, even in front of family, about my needing to be cared for throughout my life. One day, when my twin sister was home from college, in front of our mother, my father told her that she would have to take care of me when he and mother were gone because I couldn't do it myself. My mother wouldn't utter a word. She never, in front of me, spoke against what he said. She never openly disagreed with him. Only when I reminded my mother of my limitations and inabilities would she say, "Oh, you can do anything." But she never openly volunteered to encourage me. She never took me aside and encouraged me or told me I was no different from other kids. She never told me that my father was wrong about me. Because of that, I always presumed she believed about me the way my father did.

Every time I tried even to just tell my mother what my father said about me, or that he tried to prod me into an argument, she would turn away and say, "I'm sorry." By the time I was fifteen, I was depressed and felt hopeless. I began to hate myself. While my two sisters were together in my older sister's room, I would go to my room, which I shared with my twin sister, sit at the little vanity, and look at myself in the mirror and berate myself. I would ask myself why I didn't die before I was born and that I wished that I had. Days like these would multiply. And so would my self-hatred.

In my mid-teens and onward, my father would continue to nudge me and push me into arguing with him by making a snide remark about my character. I refused to argue with him because I suspected it would lead to a whipping. Not falling for his ploy didn't always work either. If I remained quiet, more often than not, he would continue to egg me on, trying to incite me, ultimately, increasing his fervor and that would lead to a whipping. In those years, as my father pushed for an argument, I would begin to cry because I knew what was coming. When he would command me to go to the kitchen, I would ask what I had done, already in tears, and he would reply, "I need to straighten you out." If my sisters were around, they would make themselves scarce. It was probably around fifteen when my mother started refusing to hear about my whippings. It wasn't an abrupt stop but a gradual thing.

It seemed like no one in the family really cared about me. I knew my mother loved me, but when I needed her in the worst of pain, she would turn from me. On my mother's days off when my father started in on me, she would go to the basement. (In hindsight, I wonder if she prayed.) Then when she knew it had ended, after the commotion a whipping made, she would come back upstairs. When I sought comfort from her, she would say, "I'm sorry," then move on. I felt lost, unloved, unimportant, separated, and stranded like there was a void encircling me.

As time moved on, I would try not to talk about it with my mother after she got home from work. What was the use? I knew she didn't want to hear it. But when a really hard whipping happened, sometimes ten whacks to my backside, I couldn't help myself. My father would throw his right hand back as far as he could and then slam it against my teenage backside. Even as a teenager, I needed comfort and reassurance that I was loved and cared for, that I was a valued part of this family. So on really bad days, I couldn't hold back the desire, the need, to seek her comfort through uncontrollable tears. But from age sixteen on, when I approached her and opened my mouth with, "Mother, Daddy…," she would throw up her hand and say, "I don't want to *hear* it. I *don't* want to hear it." Her reaction ran from hugs and assurance that I was loved as a child, to a casual "I'm sorry," as a preteen and young teen, to a refusal to hear me. "Sweep it under the rug. Ignore it—it'll go away. Just pretend it didn't happen and get over it."

My father's motto was, "Grin and bear it." So I did.

Nothing is more personal than rejection. Rejection goes to the spirit of the person, not just their soul. The spirit man is the man, the part of a person that will live on after death. Rejection is a refusal to accept the person—therefore the spirit-man. The soul is our emotions and our reasoning, our attitudes. The soul is a part of us but not the essence of us. Our souls will not live on in eternity. So being rejected is a way of casting away, not recognizing the value of the person. These people who reject you are showing you that you aren't important to them and that your value to them is limited or substandard. Your acceptance is problematic because there's just something about you that they cannot endure. Rejection is a personal refusal of who you are.

Rejection begets loneliness. The loneliness I felt grew as time went on because the rejection grew. Rejection is like ice water poured over you unexpectedly. Initially, shocking and brutal. A stark, surprising slap in the face. On the other hand, loneliness creeps up on you, like the darkness sneaks upon the daylight. You aren't fully aware of it until it has a strong, hard, and heartless grip on you, an endless, unrelenting gnawing at your heart like a raw open sore that refuses to heal. Rejection makes you feel abandoned, spurned, a burden, disavowed, unwanted. (In some cases, you're accepted unless you cause me discomfort.) Loneliness makes you feel forsaken, isolated, desolate, empty, and invisible. Both make you feel unloved, unaccepted, unimportant, and unworthy. The kind of love they have for you seems conditional, contingent on your behavior or attitude, or your cost to them.

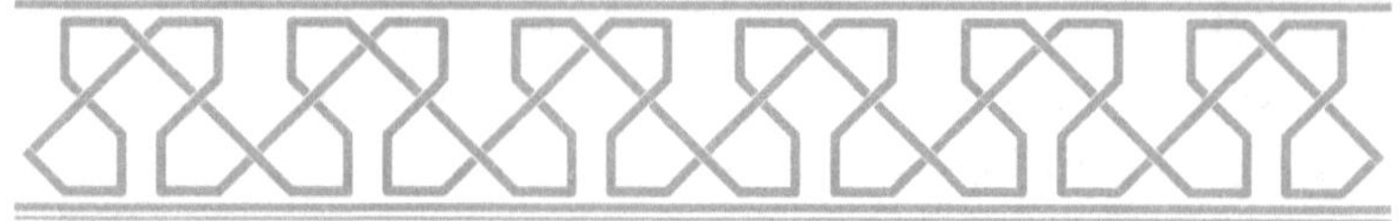

Punishment versus Correction

Punishment makes the child feel guilt and shame about what he has done. (If I had a nickel for every time my father said to me, "I'd be ashamed," I would have been a millionaire by the time I was twenty years old.) Nothing good can come out of guilt or shame. If punished often enough, the child feels guilt and shame about being himself.

My opinion of *punishment*/whippings/beatings is this: It makes the child resentful; intimidated; fearful of all authority figures; fearful of being judged; and feeling inferior, unworthy, hopeless, and unaccepted as they are, and he eventually believes he is a bad person and wrong. His innateness is wrong. Beating a child will destroy their selfness, their individuality that God put in them to make them unique, which sets them apart from everyone else. It will strip them of their true identity. It can also stifle the call that the Lord has on their life, as with me.

On the other hand, *discipline* in the form of correction focuses on correcting bad behavior. It defines the wrong and explains why it's wrong. It allows the child the opportunity or time to absorb the facts about doing the thing that has been deemed wrong. It's training the child to be able to think why this action is wrong or unacceptable. Discipline should *teach* the child good behavior, *not punish* him for the wrong. Most of what a child does that is considered wrong by a parent isn't *wrong* in and of itself. It's wrong—unacceptable to the parent. It's being a child and unlearned in good behavior. Growing up is a learning process. Children aren't born with the capacity to have adult understanding. And again, children mature differently; their understanding of behavior is different. The parent may need more patience with one child than he may need with another.

When I was a parent to my young son, and I saw things he did that I got a whipping for, I ignored them because they weren't *wrong* or *bad*; they were childish behaviors that I knew he would grow out of. When he threw a ball, and it hit the house, or when he ran under the clothesline where I had laundry hanging, I didn't call him in and whip him. The first chance I had to see him, I would say, "Don't..." and then I would let it go. He learned in time—his time—to think quickly before he ran under the clothesline full of laundry or when throwing a ball. I was much more patient and understanding with my son. Maybe coming from my past taught me that children need time to acclimate to adulthood, to adjust or adapt their thinking and behavior as they mature.

We aren't born with the knowledge or life experiences of our parents. Children are different from each other, even sisters are different from each other, and most assuredly, twins can be very different. They all learn differently and at different speeds. And we each have a specialty about us. Something unique that God put in us inadvertently drives us, motivates us, and helps make us who we are. And God has a purpose for whatever that uniqueness in us is. Punishment, especially done in anger, twists that inner self, that self-confidence, the assurance of our value, the natural trust in our abilities, the defining quality that helps make us who we are. God didn't use cookie cutters to make His children. He makes them differently, intentionally, for His specific purposes. He is a creative God; He doesn't have to resort to copies or duplicates.

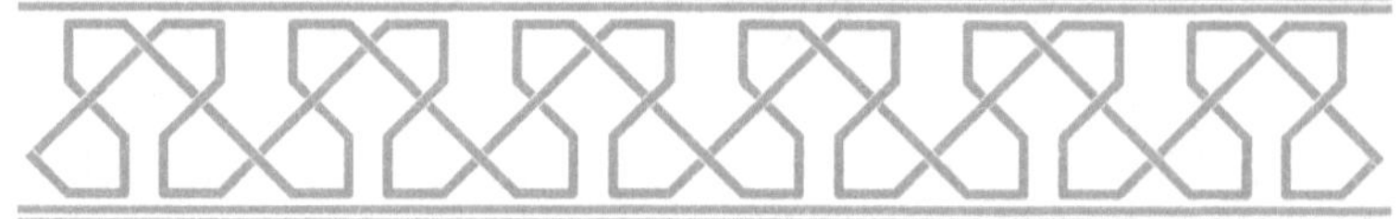

Natural Death or Suicide?

MY FATHER CONTINUED to ingrain in me that I was unable to learn, that I was defective, and that there was something deficient in me. I was missing something that would have aided my mental capabilities and my value as a daughter. So not only was I a bad, rebellious, and disrespectful person, but I was also unable to learn anything. I just needed to accept these facts. And a part of me did. But there was something deep inside me that believed differently. That had hope of the opposite.

Eventually, my time at my vanity became my time to express real hatred of myself. When my sisters would gather in my older sister's room and not include me, I would go to my room, sit at my vanity, look at my reflection, and spill out hatred for the girl who looked back at me. I would grab both hands full of my hair and pull until tears ran down my cheeks, and then say, "I hate you! I despise you! You are worthless and stupid and ugly! You're just an idiot! I wish you were dead!" I would vilify myself. I would use every negative word I could think of in my tirade. I would use the inflection of anger but in a low-key voice so that no one would hear me. Then I would go downstairs as though nothing had happened.

Around age sixteen, after I went to bed, I started asking God to let me die before morning because I couldn't stand the pain. As nights, and with the disappointment of waking the next morning, moved on, I started begging God to let me die. Even when I hadn't gotten a whipping that day, I wanted my life to be over if the pain wasn't. As was my custom, I would read my little red Bible, climb into bed, pray, and sob until I fell asleep. Every morning, I'd awaken, realize I was still in my bed, and would think, *God doesn't love me. If He did, He would let me die, or He would stop my father from hurting me.* I would get up wondering if I'd get a whipping that day and wonder for what reason. Daily, I wondered why God didn't intervene in my situation. Maybe it was because He agreed with my father. I think I had a love/hate feeling for God. I depended on Him yet feared Him. It wasn't a healthy, honorable kind of respectful fear. It was real fear, an anxiousness in my attitude toward Him. I felt so uncertain about Him. My mixed feelings were on and off, up and down toward Him. In Sunday school (Bible study), I never let anyone know my true doubts about God. Nor did I reveal to my mother or sisters my complex relationship with my heavenly Father.

Since God wouldn't let me die, maybe I should handle it myself. I wondered every night what would be the best method to handle suicide. I had a few options. My father had several guns and rifles and shotguns in the basement, but they were very securely under lock and key, as secure as Fort Knox. I knew I would never be able to obtain one. I could use a knife or a razor blade, but these two approaches would take a long time to accomplish. I believed that my twin sister would probably walk in on me before death would come, and she would call for help. When my father would find out, rather than be concerned about the why for my killing myself, I knew he would be out of control with rage, and a flogging would occur. I sincerely believed that this whipping would *kill* me. The fact that my father's actions would kill me wasn't the issue. I *dreaded* the emotional pain I would have to endure through the torture, and *that* is what would terminate my life. I couldn't fathom the grief that I would incur. That would be the ultimate heartbreak for me. I believe that my father's attitude would have been, "You want to die? I'll accommodate you." His desire to send me on my way was just too much for me to think about. I couldn't handle that heavy of a burden. Believing that I was a failure made me acutely aware of the possibility of my failure at suicide. So I continued to consider the manner in that I would choose to end my life, to end my pain.

During these intervals of indecision, I wondered which would be worse, dying by my father's hand because of my failure to succeed at suicide or my father's constant abuse. I continued to consider the forms that I could use to kill myself. But I always came back to the thought that I would fail, and my father's wrath would fall upon me. Dying was not worth the emotional pain I would have endured at my father's angry hand, no matter the duration of the punishment. That thought gave me pause.

I continued to beg God to let me die. I continued to dream about it, to make tentative plans. I thought of friends I would leave my few treasures to when I was gone. I wondered how my family would react if I died. Would they get over it quickly? Would they even notice? How would my mother feel? Would they remember me? My father probably would feel relief. "Grin and bear it," his mission statement.

No Art School

My twin sister and I started college together. My father continually reminded me that I barely graduated. Actually, I was smack-dab in the middle of a class of almost five hundred students. Could be worse. While at college, I felt like I was on a merry-go-round. I had been controlled so severely that now, I had a hard time making decisions on my own, for myself. I didn't know which way was best. I was so used to being told every move to make, I almost felt lost like there was a screw loose.

I was not satisfied in college. I didn't want a degree. I wondered what degree I would work for anyway. Nothing there fit me. I wanted to go to art school. I loved art and made really good grades in art class. I enjoyed the different types of art—painting, drawing, sculpture, and something I call reverse drawing where you melt crayons and when it cooled, you would draw on it, therefore cutting into the wax and forming a picture. But my parents wouldn't allow it. I remember asking my mother why they wouldn't let me go to art school. She had a dish towel in her hands. She fidgeted with it, shook her head, and walked away. It broke my heart. There was an art school in the city, unaccredited. I didn't require a diploma or degree to do art. Just training. I longed to go to art school. I would have to ride two city buses to and from, but since I had no funds to pay for it, and my parents wouldn't even think about it, and I didn't have the self-confidence to earn an income, the dream remained a dream. Just like Africa.

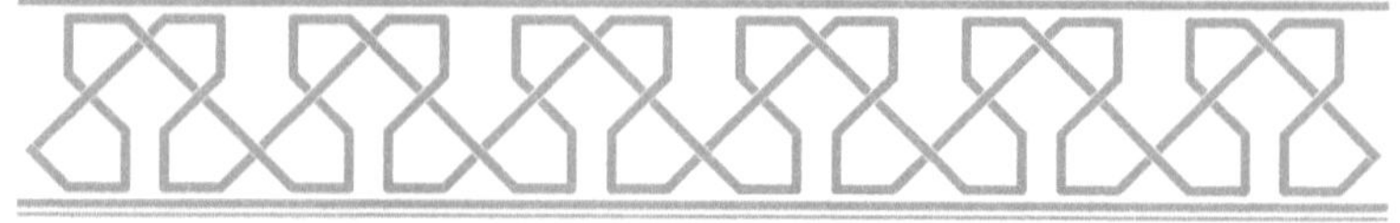

My Young Adult Years

THAT SUMMER, TWO of my friends from my year at college came by one day. They were on their way to the college campus for a couple of days. I asked permission to go. Of course, my father said, "No." No reason. Unlike my twin sister, I never asked my parents why. A very close friend suggested that maybe I should not have asked permission and gone, anyway. I told her I was afraid that my father would not let me back in the house. I was nineteen.

In the fall of the year, I looked for work. I knew that there was absolutely nothing that I could do that would earn me a paycheck. I was not good at anything. My chances of failure to do anything well were sky-high. I spent many days seeking office work, to no avail. I figured the reason I was not successful at being hired, first and foremost, was because I was a failure and because these people I spoke with about getting a job knew right off that I was a bad person who would fail at the job I would have been hired to do. After unsuccessful attempts at finding work, I would head to my vanity and denigrate myself.

One weekend, in the early fall, of my twin sister's sophomore year, she asked me to come the following weekend. I wanted to, but she told my father that she wanted me to come the next weekend, and he replied, "No, some boy would drag her off and rape her!" I have no idea what prompted that reason. My sister was speechless.

Because my older sister worked at the retail store where my mother worked, and my twin sister was a sophomore in college, I was responsible for preparing my father's lunch and the meal that he would take with him to work that evening. He complained about me not having a job, but he wouldn't help me get a job in the office of the factory where he worked. He feared that I would embarrass him.

One day in early fall, right after he finished his lunch and as I was washing the dishes, the phone rang. Because my father had malaria that he contracted while he was in the army stationed in Guadalcanal that affected his hearing, he never answered the phone. I let the big cast-iron skillet that I was scrubbing sink under the water and went to answer the phone. It was an aunt, one of my father's sisters. She's the one I believe my father went to see after my whippings. She called me to tell me that I wasn't smart enough to go to college and that I wasn't college material. Some people just don't belong at college, and I had to accept that fact. I replied, "Aunt, I don't want to go to college." I did not speak in anger. I was matter-of-fact in my reply.

Suddenly I knew my father was standing behind me. He grabbed the phone out of my hand and without asking who this was or "She'll call you back" to the caller, he said, "I'll call you back later," and he hung up the phone. I went back to the kitchen, picked up the skillet, conscious of an impending thrashing, and started scrubbing the skillet. He came up behind me, hovering over me, incensed, and said, "Don't you disrespect my sister!"

I turned toward him, trying to stay composed, knowing that I was in big trouble, and said as calmly as I could, "I didn't disrespect her."

The next thing I knew I was on the floor about two feet from where I had been standing, with a sharp sting to my cheek. My father had smacked me in the face with the back of his hand. It happened so fast that I didn't see it coming. I was beyond astounded, aghast. For a few seconds, I wondered what just happened. I wondered what was next. He left the house, probably had gone to this sister's house, and I, wailing, hurried to my room and sobbed. I just had to tell my mother, so when she got home from work, I tried, but up went that hand and her words of refusal to hear me.

Feelings of rejection and loneliness fell on me again. That raw open sore had been ripped wider. It was excruciating. I was almost at the end of my rope. I wondered what to do. I had nowhere to go. I had no one to go to. I felt like I was at a dead end and facing the devil or the deep blue sea. I saw no end to my father's abuse or my mother's rejection. I wondered what to do. Thoughts of dying came back to me.

When we three sisters were teenagers, we stayed the night with this aunt's daughter who had cerebral palsy. When I was fifteen or sixteen on one night's visit, I tried to talk to this aunt. She quickly and sternly replied, "Don't talk about your daddy that way." I never tried again.

Late one winter morning, my father told me to go to the basement. I believed he was going to whip me there so that my cries would be muffled. Maybe it was because my mother was home that day, and he didn't want her to know what he had planned for me. He told me again that I was so bad, rebellious, and disrespectful (his favorite description of me) that he couldn't do anything with me. I began to cry and asked him why he was hounding me and what it was that I did to be in trouble because we had not had an encounter or even spoken that morning. He replied, "Hounding you? I'm just trying to straighten you out." (I always wondered what about me truly needed straightening out.) I was not any of the things he described of me. I knew that in my heart. I believed all the negative words he spoke over me, but I knew that I knew that I was not bad nor did I ever treat anyone badly. He said he was going to call the police and have me taken to reform school. "Maybe they can do something with you to straighten you out." I knew that I was too old for reform school; I was nineteen.

In all the years my father whipped me, I never once said, "No." I never said, "No more." I never stood against him when he was about to throw his hand back. I just took it.

I went to church with my family or my two sisters for every event. Sunday Bible study, worship service, Sunday night service, Wednesday night prayer meeting, youth group, and youth choir. I never cussed, drank, smoked, took drugs, partied, sassed, and went anywhere without permission. I read my Bible daily and prayed every night (and many days). My sisters and I were always together, at home, shopping, or at a movie. Especially as a preteen and teenager, I did what my father asked of me. I never refused. Where he got the idea that I was bad, rebellious, and disrespectful, I truly have no idea. In the strictest of terms, my twin sister was sometimes blunt with him, but he never got on her for it. I wondered how she could tell him he was too controlling and strict and never got in trouble.

One day, she told my father that he was destroying me. He replied in shock, "Destroying her? I'm just trying to straighten her out." Then he laughed and walked away. And then she walked away. I never had the nerve to confront him about anything. I was very fearful of him and had respect for his position as my father, yet I was always in trouble.

Several times after my father's lunch and my cleaning up the kitchen, I would sit on the sofa and read or draw. He would be reading the newspaper. After a few minutes, he would make a snide comment. I ignored him. There would be a pause and more negative remarks. Sometimes I would get up and go to my room to prevent an encounter, and that would be the end of the situation. Other times, with the same scenario, when I would get up to get away from his criticism, he would call me back and say, "I'm not finished with you yet." Some of those times, he would be satisfied with berating me. Other times, he would work himself into a fever emotionally, and a whipping would result. In my late teens, my days were so uncertain. I was always aware that something or nothing would unhinge him.

One day as he finished the lunch, I had prepared for him, along with the meal he was to take to work, he said, "I don't believe you like me." I stopped, turned to look at him, then walked away. I learned several years after I married that my mother expected me to run away as a teenager. The reason I did not run away was because I knew I could not make it on my own. I had zero self-confidence. I knew either I would live on the streets or come back home, and I didn't believe my father would allow me to return.

Another *worse* whipping I suffered happened in April before my twentieth birthday in July. The whipping that left welts on my bottom as a child was done with the paddle he *made for* me. This one was by his hand. It must have stung a great deal by the time he stopped hitting me. I had pounded the pavement of places that might need office help to no avail the previous winter. One afternoon, immediately after the lunch I had prepared for my father and the meal I had prepared for him to take to work that afternoon at three-thirty, I was sitting on the sofa reading one of my mother's new magazines. My father was sitting adjacent to me, as usual. That was his chair. Again he was reading the newspaper. After a while, he made a sarcastic remark about me. I remained quiet and continued to read. He waited a few moments and spoke again. I didn't respond, but I suspected he was baiting me.

As several times before, he would turn the upper left corner of the paper down to look over it. I knew what was coming. I was afraid to get up and leave because I suspected that would anger him, so I sat there quietly. My heart started pounding. Been there, done that.

The intervals of his cynical comments and his silence became shorter, his remarks more spiteful, more derogatory. His voice got louder and raised to a higher pitch used when a person calls to someone from across the room. He was intentionally demeaning me, degrading me, cutting my character to shreds. He was determined to get a rise out of me. As every time before, I remained silent, hoping he would find his attempt to rile me futile. That didn't happen. He continued to insult me, and I began to cry.

My older sister was home that day. She heard his loud, angry voice and came to the living room to find out why my father was yelling. She asked, "What's going on?" My father explained to her that I was just sitting there doing nothing useful and that I couldn't find work because of my poor character, and started on his list of my faults. She said, "Leave her alone." He went on with his list of complaints against me. My sister suggested that he get me a job in the office of the factory where he worked. That way, "She could ride with you." (I wonder how his tirade would have ended had she not suggested that he help me get a job there.)

My father exploded. He would never want me there. They would find out what a bad person I was, and it would reflect on him. On and on he went with all the reasons he would never allow me to apply for work there or suggest me to his bosses. My sister returned to her room. I was sobbing, completely unnerved. There seemed to be no end to his criticism of me. They cut to the core. He seemed to not run out of negative words to speak over me. His ranting lasted, from his first remark to the command for me to "get to the kitchen," about thirty minutes. I stood up, shaking with sobs as I did as he commanded.

As I left the sofa, he grabbed my left wrist tight. I tried to loosen his grip because it was cutting off circulation. I told him that he was hurting me, and he replied, "I aim to hurt you." And he did just that. Usually, during my whippings, he had control of the situation and his emotions. He would strike me about ten times like he was counting. He was a precise, meticulous, non-haphazard person. Nothing he did was spontaneous or unplanned. This time was different. He lost control of his emotions. He struck at me wildly with a fierce force anywhere his hand would land. I remember putting my right hand behind me to block the strikes, and he said, "Move your hand!" I did. He struck me probably at least fifteen times. I was afraid that he was truly going to hurt me, not just with the whipping but in a way that would be a serious injury. I was wailing, and he told me to be quiet. I tried. I tried to stifle my sobs. Finally, I couldn't endure anymore, and I slumped to the floor. My father couldn't lift me up to continue, partly because of my dead weight and partly because his right arm was worn out. He turned and left the house, probably going to his sister's house, and I limped to my room, collapsing on my bed. My father picked my mother up from work when she got off. I'm sure he explained that I was out of control, and he had to straighten me out. Again, she turned away from me. Thoughts of suicide came back to me.

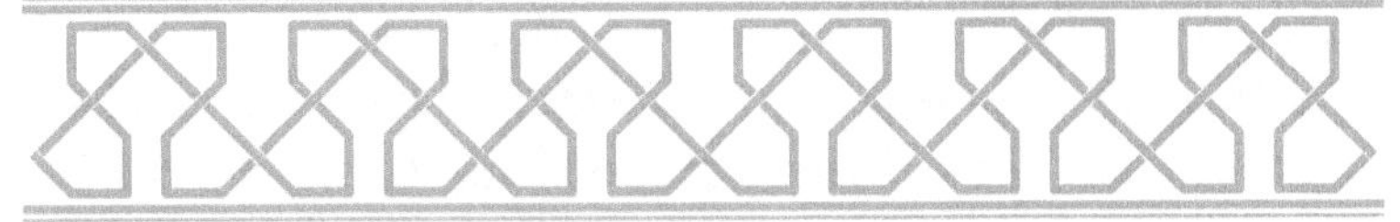

Joy and More Torment

A FEW WEEKS later, maybe out of guilt, he told my mother to ask if I wanted to go to beautician school. He was willing to pay for that but not art school. I didn't want to go, but I felt I had no other choice, so I agreed. People who suffer from inferiority and fear do not belong in a profession where you have to please someone. I was terrified of having to do exactly what the patron wanted. Fear of rejection was my constant companion. I longed for art school.

Six months later, a friend of mine and I drove my twin sister back to campus. It was a Sunday. The best thing to ever happen to me happened that day. I met the country boy I was to marry. He was a very positive, confident person. Just what I needed. His name was Kenneth. I would soon start calling him Kenny. That was Sunday, November 17, 1968. It was ten years and two days after the greatest day of my life—when I got saved.

In February of 1970, we became engaged. One evening in the spring, Kenny came to pick me up. We were going to a movie. My parents were planning a visit to one of his sisters and her husband's house where the other sister and her husband would be also. It was suggested that we join them before going to the movie. We agreed. When we arrived, everyone was taking a seat in the backyard. After everyone was seated, there was only one remaining chair. I don't know how my father would be unaware of it. Kenny and I hesitated, not knowing exactly what to do. Finally, Kenny said, "I'll sit, and you sit on my lap." He sat in the remaining chair, and I sat on his knee. I said, I sat on Kenny's *knee*, not his *lap*. I sat straight up on his knee. My father jumped up from his chair, stormed over to Kenny and me, thrust his finger at me, and commanded, "Get out of his lap!" I was dumbstruck. Without a peep, I jumped up. Kenny didn't know what to do. I had described my father's and my relationship to him, so he knew of my father's outbursts and abuse.

My father loomed over me; he went ballistic, scorning me in front of everyone, loud and almost out of control. I believe this was the angriest that I ever saw my father. Everyone was seated when Kenny took a seat, and it was obvious there were limited chairs. Everyone there sat stunned into silence. I was scorched, humiliated, and shamed. I looked at my mother. She seemed unfazed. The uncle who lived in the house brought a chair from the kitchen, and I sat in it. The two aunts and uncles made light of the situation, trying to defuse my father. Soon Kenny and I left. After we got in Kenny's 1965 Ford Fairlane, he indicated that we should have left immediately. I explained that many times when I thought my father's rant had ended, and I turned to leave, he would demand that I come back, "I'm not through with you." So I feared that my father would do the same in this incident. I just wanted to leave.

When my father bought my older sister a car and refused to allow my twin sister and me to get our own driving licenses, he told us that when we needed to go somewhere, our sister would drive us. That did not happen. Both of Kenny's parents had already passed, so because he was a senior in college and working, I was responsible for planning our wedding. One day I asked my sister to drive me to different florists so I could check on flowers for my wedding. She denied me that request. I told my mother, believing she would uphold my father's promise. She didn't. She replied, "It's not her place to drive you around." A little later, I was discussing my plans with my mother, expecting advice, when she commented, "It's not right for the younger sister to get married before the older one does." I was deflated. Another rejection. A double standard. I reasoned that she would be glad for me to marry first and right away so I would leave the nest, and their home would be quiet. I'm sure their home was much more peaceful after I left.

In hindsight, I wonder if my father regretted not having someone to criticize and demean.

There seemed to always be a double standard in our home. My father was livid over me sitting on Kenny's knee but much more indulgent with both my sisters. Soon after Kenny and I were married, one evening I called my mother, and she made the comment that my sister (I'll not say which one) was lying on the sofa with her boyfriend as they and my parents watched television. I reminded my mother of the way my father reacted concerning my sitting on Kenny's knee and my sister lying with her boyfriend. "Why the difference?" I asked her. She brushed it off.

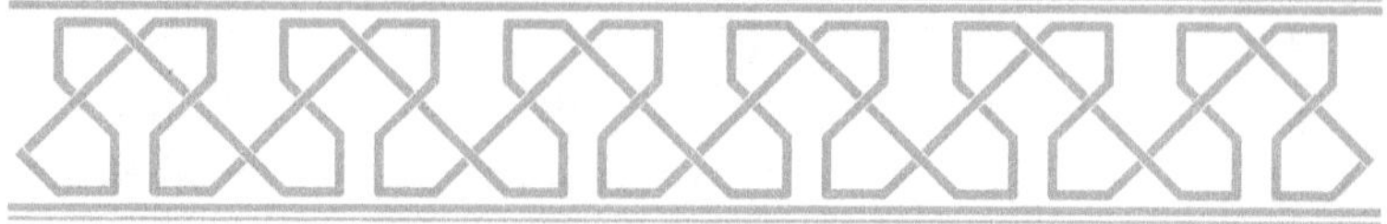

Early Married Years

AFTER OUR WEDDING, we moved north where Kenny had worked in the summer while he was attending college, and we lived there for two years before moving south. Three years later, we moved in with his just-widowed grandfather on his farm in south-central Kentucky because there was no one to care for him. Soon after that move, I began having dreams about my father. The subject matter was always the same. My twin sister and I were on the sidewalk of a high school or a college building about to go in when my father would appear. He would, in a matter-of-fact manner, remind me that I would fail, that learning was too difficult for me, and that I needed to give up and come home. My sister would insist that I could do it. "Come on." I would then awaken. This dream came to me regularly, for many, many years.

When Kenny and I found out that we were going to have a baby, we invited my parents to come for a visit. After the initial greetings, I took my mother into my bedroom and handed her a little gift box tied with ribbon. When she opened it, she discovered a pair of white baby shoes. She smiled and then said, "Your daddy never loved you." (Tell me something I don't know.) I asked her why, and she replied, "I don't know." Nothing was spoken about the subject ever, ever again.

When I became pregnant, my general practitioner sent me to an ob-gyn in a town thirty-five miles away. There were three doctors who shared their patients. On one of my visits, while I was still on the examining table, the doctor who was attending to me on that visit sexually assaulted me. I kept wondering where the nurse was and when she was coming back into the examining room. She never did. As he assaulted me, he looked right at me. I turned from his look, covered my face with my left arm, and wept. When he finished, he said, "You can get dressed." I was shattered, debased, and demoralized. I hoped at my next appointment that I would not be treated by this doctor, and to my joy, when I went back, this doctor had left the practice. I never told Kenny. What could he do? It was my word against the doctor's word. I never told anyone until I shared it with a Bible teacher at a women's conference in 2019, forty-four years later.

I had wanted a couple of kids, though I never gave it a lot of thought. After our son was born, I felt such deep emotions of joy and fulfillment. I had a wonderful husband and a beautiful child. But I also felt deep fear. I felt like God didn't want me this happy, and if I pushed my luck, He might take one of these loved ones from me. I never ever told anyone about this.

Many days, I would sit and write about my pain, the dark oppression that I still was feeling, on notebook paper. I would write until I felt drained. Then I would go do my household chores. Later in the day, I would go back and read what I had written, and as was so customary for me, I sobbed. Then I would destroy the papers I had written on. I didn't want Kenny to know about it. I never told him.

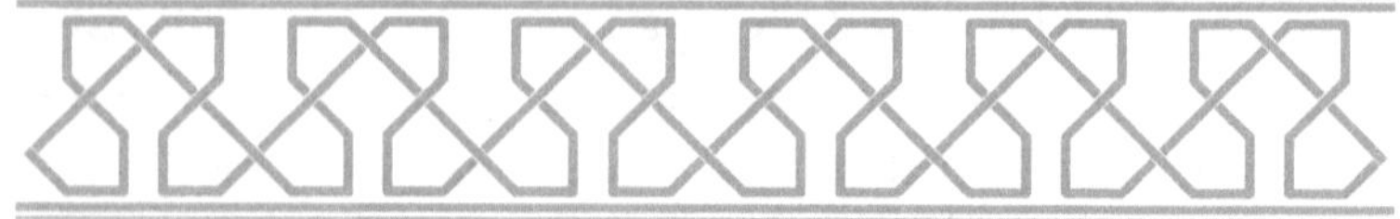

An Angel's Visit

ONE DAY, DURING the warm months of 1982, I was lying on the sofa looking out the front door. It was a beautiful day. The sofa was situated across the living room floor in the middle of the floor so that when you lay on it facing the door, you could see outside. Suddenly, I felt something, a presence. I turned to look over the back of the sofa without rising, and there stood an angel. I looked directly into his face. He was wearing a white pullover robe which had a gold braided belt. The belt went around his waist, then another rope belt criss-crossed above the single rope. He had very dark hair that hung in big, loose curls that rested on his shoulders. I can no longer describe his face, but I do remember he was very handsome. He spoke to me. This is what he said, "Preach, teach, and believe." I blinked. He was gone. I was stunned, to say the least, partly by seeing an angel but mostly by what he said to me. This rejected person, who was told so many times that she was mentally deficient, would always be a failure, would never be able to take care of herself, just saw an angel, *and* he *spoke* to her. Did God really tell me to preach, teach, and believe? Me? Indeed, He did. I told my best friends and my mother. My mother was thrilled. I don't know if it was because an angel actually appeared in my house and spoke to me or if it was what he told me. Other than those people, I never told anyone else because I figured they wouldn't believe me. They would probably tell me it was just a dream. But it was real.

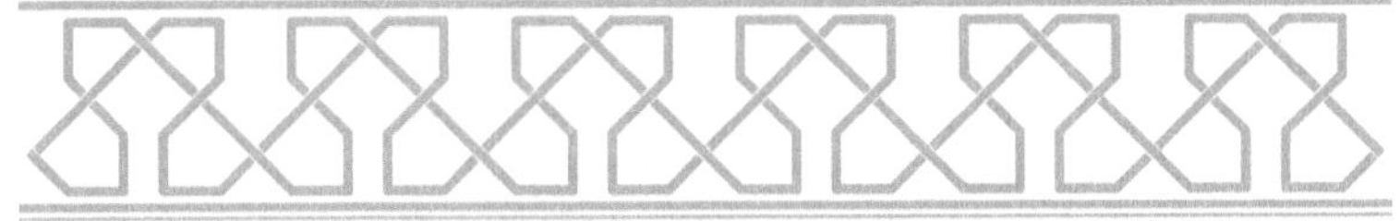

Memories Bring Torment

While Kenny was working on the farm, sometimes I would be asked to make phone calls for him. I dreaded that. Fear is illogical. It is a shallow, false emotion based on the unknown. It would take me several hours to make a call. I would start to dial the phone (rotary phones), and before I completed the number, I would hang up the phone. What if the person who answered found out I was dumb? What if I made a mistake? What if I get a wrong number? What if I didn't know exactly what to say?" What if…? I would do something, like close a window or put my keys in my purse, and then go back and check several times. When we were kids, my twin sister and I were told to close the window and storm window when we were leaving for a trip out of town. We would do so, then my father would tell us to go back and check to make sure we did it. We would go back and check and confirm it was done, but we'd be told to go back and check again. We would do so. Then my father would go check to make sure we did as we were told to do two or three times. This was another reason why I was always so very unsure of myself. Kenny was very encouraging and positive, but I thought that was only because he loved me.

To give an idea of the depth of my illogical fear—after the mail ran, I would walk out onto the front porch and listen for traffic. If I heard a vehicle coming from a couple of miles away, I would stay on the porch. If I heard nothing, I would head for the mailbox about one hundred twenty feet from the house. If I heard a vehicle approaching en route to the mailbox, I would stop by the car parked in the semicircular drive or dart into the garage Kenny's grandfather used. After it passed, I would hurry to get the mail and then hurry back to the house. The spirit of fear makes you fear anything for absolutely no reason. After the spirit of rejection, the spirit of fear was the worst in power and strength over me. It was the last to leave. (But I think he left a few small cohorts.)

Both of my sisters lived (and live) in our hometown, ninety miles from where I live. When the three of us, or just my twin sister and I, got together to shop and go to lunch or dinner, I deferred to my twin sister to speak for me. If we were shopping and I couldn't find something in my preferred color or size, I would move on. My sister would find a sales clerk and ask about the item for me. When I had a question about a menu, I wouldn't ask about the dish I wanted. But my sister would ask for me. I lived in a prison of fear.

In September of 1986, I felt like I had reached the end of my rope. The memories magnified. I could still, after all those years (sixteen and a half), feel the sting on my backside. I felt a darkness, a cloudiness encircle me. I was depressed more often than not. I tried to not let Kenny know about any of this. Coming from a completely different home environment, I didn't think he could fully understand. And what could he do about it? I was folding laundry. I said, "God, I can't do this anymore. If You don't do something, I'm going to die, and no one will know how I died."

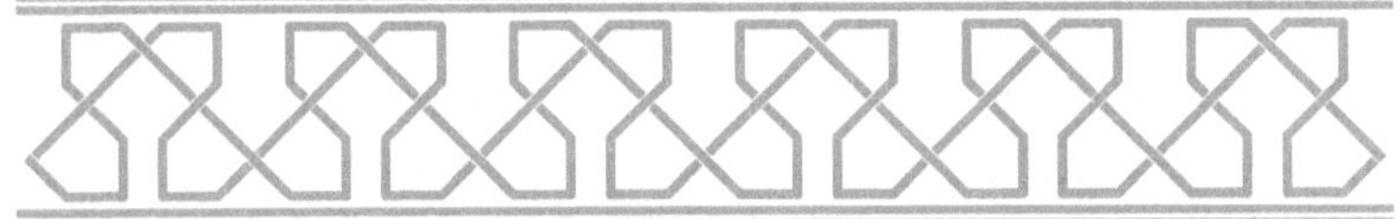

Deliverance

THE FOLLOWING DECEMBER, I remembered the friend who had introduced the Holy Spirit to me in February 1980. I trusted her, her wisdom, and her spiritual knowledge. I went to her house every two or three weeks to unload, but when she would say, "Talk to me," I would burst into tears.

Through those sobs, all I could say was, "There's so much inside me, but I can't get it out," and, "There's this person inside me. I don't know who she is." I felt like the other person inside me wasn't right, wasn't the real me, and didn't belong there. She and I were very different. I didn't know what to do about her. My friend presumed it was demonic, so she ultimately suggested I get a book about deliverance. She told me which one to buy: *Healing the Wounded Spirit* by John and Paula Sandford. (Another good book on deliverance is *The Bondage Breaker* by Neil T. Anderson.) It was a lifesaver for me, a rope thrown for someone overboard.

The next evening, on his way home from work, Kenny picked up a copy for me. He got home at nine that night. I fed him his supper and then started reading the book. I read until two thirty the next morning, then around nine or ten o'clock, I called this friend and said, "I want it." She knew what I was referring to. She contacted her friend who was, and still is, a deliverance minister, and they worked on a plan to schedule a time to minister to me.

That day came on April 11, 1987, at four o'clock in the afternoon. It was a Saturday. I was asked to describe some of my attitudes—disappointments and letdowns. My friend asked the minister what she thought, and she replied, "I see *rejection*." I wondered how she figured that out. My husband's grandfather was watching television in the den, so the minister suggested we go to a friend's house for ministry, which we did. In this case, my friend said she felt like the Lord wanted me to lie on the floor. After I laid down, the minister commanded the spirit of rejection to "come out of her!" She was not loud; she didn't holler or get angry; she just firmly and confidently commanded it to leave. It did. I knew immediately that it left because I saw it. Later, I told my friend that I had seen the spirit, learning the term *manifested itself*, and she replied that the two of them also saw it. I knew the spirit was gone not only because I felt it leave but also because I saw it go out from me.

Demons Are Real

DEMONIC SPIRITS CANNOT exist in the spirit of man because the spirit is the person, the part of man that is connected to God. It is what lives forever. It's where Jesus resides in us. He will not cohabitate with a demonic spirit. Demonic spirits have no authority over the spirit man. These evil spirits can and do live in the soul area. Our souls consist of our attitudes, emotions, and our will. There are conflicting beliefs in the church about demonic spirits residing in or possessing Christians.

In Hebrew, there are two definitions of *possession.* One definition means to own, to have legal authority over or a legal right to something or some place. The other one refers to taking over, manipulating, or controlling what is not rightfully their own. I know from experience that they can inhabit Christians. I actually saw one leave my body, so I know it's true. I've had a lot of deliverance, but the spirit of rejection is the only one that manifested. Demonic spirits are attached to sins and negativity. They can gain access through generational sin, voluntary sin, sexual sin, and sin perpetrated by someone on another person such as any sexual assault, misconduct, or exploitation including sexual abuse, sexual molestation, rape, or incest. They also enter through negative and critical words spoken over someone. In this case, if the person *hearing* the judgmental, merciless words *believes* the words, a door is opened to receive that negativity, that condescension. When we believe or accept the person's *opinion* of us, their words of our *worth*, into our hearts, we are opening that door to allow the negative spirits into our lives. Whether it's psychological abuse, sexual abuse, or physical abuse, the demon has access. It doesn't seem fair that we would be affected by demonic oppression as children because someone exploited us, does it?

Demons believe that once they have entered the child's soul, they have that child for life. Unfortunately, often they do. People who have authority over us as children can cause us to become victims of their mistreatment and disregard, even their neglect. Because we are subject to them, to their position, we trust them or fear them and learn to accept the abuse committed against us, ultimately believing it. Demonic influence is also involved in bullying because often we accept and believe their attitude toward us, with or without physical beatings.

Accepting the abuse, whatever kind, believing we are what they say we are or we deserve what they do to us, opens the door to their entrance. Our emotions are the way we receive or deny their entrance into our lives. If we fight, psychologically, mentally, against the treatment or words, if we refuse to believe the abuser's belief of who and what we are, we can better endure their mistreatment of us and keep the demonic spirits out of our soul area, even as the abuse continues.

The demonic spirits that entered me came in through my ears. I heard the criticism and verbal assaults and believed them then accepted them as truth. Why would my father lie to me? Refusing to believe our value in the perpetrator's opinion, even as we are victims of abuse in the natural, at that time, helps us keep the door to demonic spirits closed. Curses have no power that we don't give them. When we believe them, we give them our power.

The demons who are attached to verbal abuse enter the child through their ears. The child hears and believes then accepts the negative words spoken over them, like I did. I got saved when I was ten years old but had already accepted the judgmental and cynical attitude of my father. The demons did not leave when I got saved because I had invited them in with my acceptance of them. They had legal ground to my soul. I believe there is a demon connected to each critical, abrasive word, in every language.

Life and Death Are in the
Power of the Tongue

Words can build you up or tear you down; they can break your heart or edify you. They can discourage you or encourage you.

> A gentle tongue is a tree of life but perverseness in it breaks the spirit. (Proverbs 15:4 ASV)

How true this is. Has your spirit been broken? Abuse of any kind can break a child's spirit. It takes away their hope and deadens their self-value.

> Mean-spirited slander is heartless. (Proverbs 18:21 TMG)

Some commentaries say the person who speaks death or life will reap the repercussions. Other commentaries say the person who hears the words, believes the words of death or life, and accepts them as truth will eat whichever fruit they choose to believe and accept. It's our choice to accept words of life or words of death. As children, we don't know to make a choice of what to accept, but as adults, we have enough life experiences to know what to accept and what to deny.

Either way, negative, blistering, discouraging words hurt, and encouraging, helpful, and loving words bless.

Parents and those in authority over children have the responsibility to make the child feel accepted, valued, and confident of their chances of success later in life. Parents need to measure the discipline of the child with the seriousness of the offense or wrongdoing done by the child.

James 3:5 says,

> So also the tongue is a small part of the body and yet it boasts of great things. See how great a forest is set aflame by such a small fire.

Lives can be ruined and destroyed by someone's tongue. Was yours? Verses 8 and 9 of the same chapter say,

> But no one can tame the tongue; it is a restless evil full of deadly poison. With it we bless our Lord and Father and with it we curse human beings who have been made in God's likeness.

Powerful, huh? By criticizing and judging someone, we are cursing them and condemning them. In essence, we are saying that God didn't do well in creating this person, and we need to make them better or right. We are usurping God's place and authority.

Because my father had constantly compared me with my twin sister all the while we were growing up, I tried to be like her, except intellectually—I knew that was futile. I tried to like what she liked, dislike what she disliked, and share her interests and opinions. But they just didn't fit. She and I were very different. I felt guilty about not being like her. I felt estranged from "rightness," from being "okay." (I also felt ashamed of not knowing things that perhaps I should have known. That lasted for years.) Apparently, because we were twins, even though fraternal, we were supposed to be alike, the same inside. To make this clear, I was supposed to be like her, not her being like me. But I had failed my father. Again.

God puts different traits, specific features, and gifts inside each of His creations for a purpose. His intentions are that we all be unique. If we were all alike, only the same things in God's kingdom would get done because we'd all see the same needs and issues in people, the church, and the world. We all would gravitate toward one particular goal, leaving the rest of our needs unmet. It would result in an unbalanced kingdom. God has a specific responsibility for each of us. He knew us in our mother's womb. Actually, He knew us before we were conceived (Jeremiah 1:4–5, as I mentioned earlier in this book).

> For You, O Lord, are my hope, my trust, O Lord, from my youth. Upon You I have leaned from *before* my birth. You are He who took me from my mother's womb. (Psalm 71:5–6 ESV)

> I praise You, for I am fearfully and wonderfully made. (Psalm 139:14 NKJV)

I guess my father didn't know this scripture.

> For You formed my inward parts; You covered me in my mother's womb. I will praise You, for I am fearfully and wonderfully made. Marvelous are Your works, And *that* my soul knows very

well. My frame was not hidden from You, when I was made in secret. And *skillfully* wrought in the lowest part of the earth. Your eyes saw my substance, being yet unformed. And *in Your book they were all written, the days fashioned for me, when as yet there were none of them.* (Psalm 139:13–16 NKJV; italics mine)

God has our days numbered, ordained, and planned out. No one is an accident or a mistake. No one is wrong in and of themselves. No one is useless. No one is haphazard. No one has the right to undo what God did and then try to redo the person his own way. God gives each of His children all the attributes that He wants in them—and that includes you. God is about life. God is about purpose. God is about love. God is love.

I experienced deliverance many times over the next seven or eight years. Most of my deliverance was orchestrated by my now-co-pastor's aunt. All of the spirits had to do with negative self-image emotions: failure, ineptness, fear, inferiority, unworthiness, being a burden, and of course, rejection.

My last deliverance occurred in September 1995 or 1996. The pastor of the church Kenny and I attended had asked an evangelist to come speak a few nights a week. The evangelist also did deliverance ministry. One night, I was sitting in the back of the sanctuary with some friends. This evangelist was speaking as he walked across the front of the church. He turned, caught my glance, and without skipping a beat, began walking back to the center of the front. Immediately after he caught my glance, he started telling the congregation that there was someone there who had been called to be a missionary but felt too dumb to do so. Even though a couple of women went forward, I knew he was referring to me because he was looking right at me. Suddenly, my physical strength drained out of me. My legs became wobbly, and my heart pounded harder than ever before, but I stood and went down front, and he prayed for me. I sobbed but felt a release of something heavy that had been on me.

Demons and Christians

DEMONS WHO ATTACH themselves to the sins of the perpetrator or the victim continue to try to control the person as they mature. This is a common reason young women who are victims of any kind of sexual abuse get involved in promiscuity and enter the sexual entertainment industry.

Demons won't leave their *residence* just because you want them to or just because you tell them to. They will leave only when commanded to leave in the *name* of *Jesus*. The person doing the commanding has to exert power and authority and have confidence in the *power* of Jesus's name. The oppressed or possessed person must renounce the demon.

Once a person is freed from the demonic spirit, they must renew their minds. That means rethinking what you've been thinking about yourself. You do that by reading and believing God's Word. You sometimes have to force yourself to accept what God says about you in His Word. God wouldn't lie about or exaggerate His feelings toward you. He loves you with an everlasting love. Nothing will change that no matter what you do. I had a really difficult time believing that God had a personal love for me. But there is no scripture that tells us that only some people are unworthy of His love.

> God is not a man that He should lie nor
> a son of man that He should repent.
> (Numbers 23:19 NKJV)

He doesn't deceive us, nor does He change His mind about loving us. What He wrote in His Word still stands after all the passing centuries. I was struck with awe. This God, who created the universe, who scattered the stars and every planet in the sky, who ordained every living being, this God, who sent His Only Begotten Son to die for the sins of every single person, *intentionally* created me for a purpose and loved me for me. How absolutely awesome! And He feels the same way about you and everyone else.

One of my favorite scriptures is Isaiah 61:1. It says it all. God's Word can be described in this one scripture. Jesus is saying,

> The Spirit of the Lord is upon Me because the Lord has anointed Me to bring good news to the *afflicted*; He has sent Me to bind up the *brokenhearted*, to proclaim *liberty* to *captives* and *freedom* to *prisoners*.

What better, what greater news could there possibly be?

Most churches don't believe there is a thing called *deliverance* except deliverance from sin. There are many examples of Jesus delivering people from demonic oppression written about in the four Gospels. I've listed several for easy reference: Matthew 1:39, Matthew 8:16, Mark 1:34, Mark 8:31, Luke 4:35, Luke 11:14, and Luke 13:32. Every gift that God has given us is believed and supported in most churches today: salvation, the infilling of the Holy Spirit, healing, mercy, grace, forgiveness of sin, love, prosperity, answered prayer, and more. Why leave out deliverance? In my opinion, deliverance is right behind salvation in importance. Being controlled or influenced by demonic forces can disable you. It can paralyze you. It can affect every part of your life. Only deliverance can free you.

Nowhere in the Bible does God tell us that deliverance from the demonic ended after Christ died and was resurrected. His followers continued to deliver people from oppression and possession. The scripture in Ephesians 6:12 tells us that we will wrestle against the enemy. That's not referring to the unsaved—it's referring to followers of Christ. Maybe church leaders believe that spiritual deliverance is no longer relevant. But at this time in all of history, because the enemy knows his time is short, he has intensified his work to keep the unsaved blind to salvation and truth and Christians imprisoned by their past. Satan's power is in deception, lies, and the twisting of truth. Jesus's power is truth and love. Jesus is the way, the truth, the life. If the enemy can convince us that God doesn't love us or care about our lives, as he did with me, he gains a foothold. Satan doesn't just lie; he is a lie. He is the *father* of lies (John 8:44). Another reason the enemy tortures Christians is to keep them from fulfilling the call God put on their lives, like with me.

When deliverance happens to you, you know it's real and that God has truly set you free. You feel darkness lift and dissipate like fog. It's like when a cloud covering the sun, causing shadows, suddenly passes the sun, and the sun shines brilliantly on you. Spiritual deliverance is like walking out of a prison into freedom. It is literally stepping out of darkness into light—God's light, which is the brightest, cleanest, clearest, purest, warmest kind of light there is.

New Christians and young Christians may need deliverance if they come out of a traumatic environment, such as myself, or if they have a history of being involved in the occult. Sometimes the effects or results of demonic influence, like fear, inferiority, control, pride, self-righteousness, and others, appear as character flaws. The truth is that these attitudes are instilled in us; we are conditioned to accept them through people in our lives, by demonic spirits. So many people, even Christians, believe that demons vaguely entice man to sin. They are not aware of the great expanse and intensity of demonic activity except in the worst of scenarios. Satan has no authority over us except the authority that *we give him, usually* unknowingly. He wants us to continue living in the past with our mistakes, sins, failures, pain, and poor self-image. Even mature Christians can be *oppressed,* maybe even *possessed* by demonic forces, and not know it.

Any bondage is a prison that prevents a person from reaching their full, God-given role. When we are in any kind of bondage, we are slaves to it, whether a habit, an addiction, a negative attitude, or even self-hatred. I was fully controlled by fear. It prevented me from doing many things, many kinds of things that would have added to the quality of my life. So as a kid and as a wife, I sat on the sidelines for fear of failing.

Deliverance is instantaneous. Renewing the mind is a long, sometimes agonizing process. You have to unlearn all the negative things you've been told and believed about yourself. It's a roller-coaster ride, with many ups and downs. Many more downs at first. Sometimes it really is hard to accept God's *unconditional* love and acceptance. Is it really unconditional? *Yes, it is.*

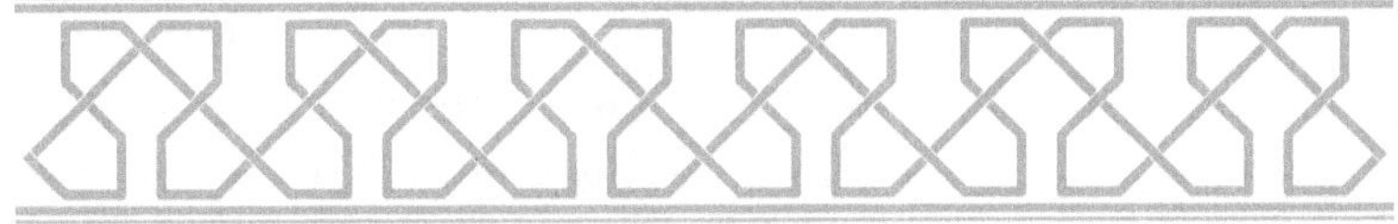

My Father's Passing and a Healing

FOUR MONTHS AFTER my first deliverance, I received a phone call from my twin sister. My father was in the hospital, diagnosed with lung cancer. He had taken radiation, to no avail. He quit smoking when he was sixty years old; he was now seventy, and the deadly disease was winning. My husband and I went to see him the next day. When we arrived, he was alone. I went to the other side of the bed and began adjusting his pillow. He said, "Don't do that. It's in my bones," meaning moving caused him great pain. There was no anger in his voice. Kenny and I stayed until evening and then went home.

A few days later, my twin sister called again. She said, "You'd better get up here." The next day, my husband, son, and I went to see my father. I knew this was the last time my son would see his pepaw. When we arrived, my mother and older sister were there. As we greeted one another, it roused my father. I walked softly to the other side of the bed. Suddenly, emotion filled my whole being, and the words, "I love you, Daddy," spilled out of my mouth.

To my surprise, he replied, "I love you, too, My."

My was the nickname he always used; very seldom did he use my given name. On his last day, my older sister's husband kept their daughter and my son while the rest of us— my husband, mother, two sisters, and I—sat with my father. He passed on August 22, 1987, four months and eleven days after my first deliverance. No coincidence, I think. I

77

wept for my mother. I wept for his grandchildren. I wept for what was and what could have been. Actually, I sobbed. The friend who was involved in my deliverance said that probably my deliverance brought deliverance to my father, as well as myself. Perhaps. I hope so. God gave us the opportunity to make things right. For that, I am eternally grateful.

Then I learned that I had to forgive my earthly father to be completely set free. After that comes healing. One morning, I was alone. I knew God had been dealing with me about forgiving my earthly father. It had been four or five years since my father's passing. I guess God thought it was high time that I did. I didn't want to. I was angry. I resented God's request of me. My father didn't deserve my forgiveness. I asked my heavenly Father why I should forgive my earthly father. My father didn't just wrong me; he intentionally berated, criticized, and whipped me for twenty out of the twenty-two years I lived under his roof. I felt like God was asking too much of me. He wasn't being fair to me. Didn't He remember how abusive my father had been to me? Didn't He see the effects of the abuse, the results that had so handicapped me and disabled me from fully functioning and having a normal life? Was He out of the office when the beatings and berating took place? (Tongue-in-cheek.) It seemed to me that forgiving my father was the same as saying, "It's okay. No harm done." God didn't reply in words. A feeling of realization came over me. I just knew that I had to do it. So I did. I forgave my father's abuse toward me. I wasn't happy to do it. I felt shortchanged and cheated. I felt no relief afterward. But in time, I saw a change in myself. I had released my resentment, bitterness, and anger toward him. Then very slowly, healing began. Eventually, the dreams ended. The memories didn't cause as much pain, but it took a long while for the pain from those memories to stop. The sting from the slaps on my backside began to fade. I didn't dwell on the past;

I didn't intentionally think about the abuse, so the thoughts about them dwindled. Now when I recall events, instances of the physical or verbal abuse, there is only regret and a wonder of how things could have been.

Forgiving and Forgetting

I CONDUCTED A study much later on forgiving and forgetting. What I learned was that when we refuse to forgive someone for their offense toward us, we are trying to *force* them to apologize. We demand that they make it right with us, believing we are not satisfied until we get justice. We think we are holding the offender hostage when, in truth, we are holding *ourselves* hostage. Some believe we must not forgive until the offender asks us to because God doesn't forgive us until we ask Him to forgive us. This belief suggests we have a biblical, *legal* right to hold out for an apology, comparing our importance to God's. He is the Creator; we are His creation. He doesn't answer to anyone, but we answer to Him. He is the *Superior* forgiving the *inferior*. So when we refuse to forgive, we are putting ourselves in the *Superior* position and the *offender* in the *inferior* position, insisting they ask for forgiveness before we grant it.

Forgiving doesn't require that we buddy up to the offender, but it aids in our healing and restoration. It softens the pain, causes the memories to fade, and speeds up the passing of resentment and bitterness. When we hear the person's name, we no longer cringe. Dreams dissipate. It allows us to move forward without hanging on to the past. God's Word commands us to forgive if we want God to forgive us.

> For if you forgive other people when they
> sin against you, your Heavenly Father
> will also forgive you. But if you do not
> forgive others their sin your Father will
> not forgive your sins. (Matthew 6:14–15
> NIV)

We must remember, we, too, sin against others and God. We are *not* without sin. Our small sins are more of an affront to the nostrils of God than someone else's sin is to ours. God is so holy, righteous, and perfect that our smallest sins are an affront to Him.

Not forgiving someone keeps the offense alive and raw, which some people desire. They want to remind you of the offense done to them. Maybe that's because they believe you will develop a hard heart toward their offender as well. Forgiving is an act of *our will.* It won't come unless we purposefully act on it. Being unforgiving can affect our health and our relationships, even the ones we have with God. If we continue to talk about an offense perpetrated against us many years ago, then we haven't forgiven the offender nor have we experienced healing. Sometimes the person says they can't forgive when in truth they *refuse* to forgive. Sometimes people feel like the offense committed against them is too big to forgive. What about our sin against God?

In the early 1990s, I was a part of a women's ministry group at my church. We met on Tuesday mornings. It was started as a prayer meeting for intercessory prayer. Soon we added Bible lessons and then included testimonies in our meetings. Every week, one of us would have a word or a message from scripture that we believed the Lord wanted us to share with the group, or one of us would share our testimony. For one meeting, one of the women had a word from Ezekiel 36:33–36. The book of Ezekiel is not a common book to use for a lesson in a Bible study, but God knows what's needed. Little did this lovely lady realize the impact this scripture would make on my life. The particular Bible version I used at that time was the New International Version. I turned to the designated scripture and followed along. However, during my reading, God replaced some of the words that are actually written in the Bible passages to fit my situation of renewing my mind. I wrote the replacement words as I read them. The following is the scripture according to the New King James Version, with my version following: Thus says the Lord God,

> On the day that I cleanse you from all your iniquities, I will also enable you to dwell in the cities, and the ruins shall be rebuilt. The desolate land shall be tilled instead of lying desolate in the sight of all who pass by. So they will say, "This land that was so desolate has become like the garden of Eden; and the wasted, desolate, and ruined cities are now fortified and inhabited." Then the nations which are left all around you shall know that I, the Lord, have rebuilt the ruined places, and planted what was desolate. I, the Lord, have spoken it, and I will do it.

My personal version:

> On the day I cleanse you from all your *sins*, I will *resettle your thinking*, and your *attitude* will be *rebuilt*. Your desolate *soul* will be *cultivated* instead of lying desolate in the sight of all who pass by you. So they will say, "This *life* that was *laid waste*

has become like the garden of Eden; the *hopes* that were *lying in ruins*, desolate and destroyed, are now fortified and active." Then the people around you that remain will know that I, the Lord, have rebuilt the *life that was destroyed* and have *replanted* the *dreams* that were desolate. I, the Lord, have spoken, and I will do it. (Emphasis mine)

It was surreal. As this woman would read, I would actually see a different word or phrase throughout the scripture. When I read my version, it made great sense to me. I thought the promise was beautiful, and it made me hopeful for a full recovery of my mindset.

A merry heart is good medicine. But a broken spirit dries the bones. (Proverbs 17:22 ESV)

Hope deferred makes the heart sick. But when the desire comes, it is a tree of life. (Proverbs 13:12 NKJV)

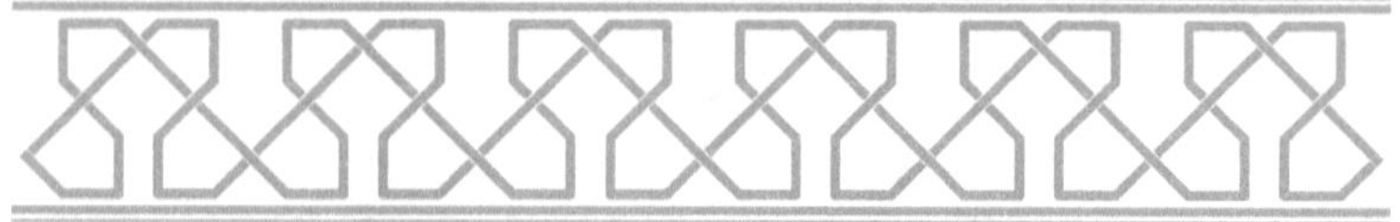

Renewing the Mind

PSYCHOLOGICAL RESTORATION TAKES time. You have to undo what's been done to you. Psychological abuse is like brainwashing, and you have to reverse it. You have to retrain your thinking about yourself,

> Be transformed by the renewing of the
> mind. (Romans 12:2 NKJV)

It is essential that we *renew* our minds. Deliverance is half the battle, and it is instantaneous, but the rethinking of yourself, your characteristics and qualities, and your value as a human being can take your whole lifetime. If we don't renew our minds, attitudes, and beliefs about ourselves by the "washing of the Word," bathing in it, drinking it, feeding on it, and filling up our minds and hearts with what God says about us, then the demons that were forced out will see the empty spaces and vacant places where they *lived* and decide to come back. And the Word says that these demons will bring *many, many* more demons with them (Matthew 12:43–45). No one wants that.

The purpose of renewing the mind is to cause us to know who we really are in Christ and become comfortable with the *new me*. God customizes each of His creations. We may be similar, but we are still unique. Nothing about us is accidental, a mistake, or wrong. I was given all the qualifications God saw that I needed to fulfill the call on my life. And so were you. God is love. God is about life and an abundant life for His children.

Another of my favorite scriptures is John 8:31–32. It says,

> If you continue (abide) in my Word, you are my disciples, indeed. And you shall know the *Truth* (Jesus) and the *Truth* (Jesus) shall make you *free*.

If you stay in His Word, you will get to know Him and realize that He loves you with everlasting love. You also will gain more freedom from not only your pain but your sin too. I learned that believing all the negative words my father spoke over me and to me was also a sin. Because I believed lies.

I had conflicting emotions trying to rule my decisions and actions for a number of years after all of my deliverance, and in between. I tiptoed into the reestablishment of my thoughts, attitudes, and opinions of myself. It's difficult to believe positive words and descriptions of yourself when you have a history of negativity. I gradually tested my self-confidence, reevaluating my mental acuity and capabilities. Often my eyes would tear up when I felt cornered, even in the company of people that I knew cared about me. When I got home, I wept. Those episodes finally ended.

Our tears, though, are in themselves, healing for us. Each time we cry, we are removing a layer of pain. One dear friend, who is now with Jesus, told me, "Crying is like peeling back layers of an onion." One crying spree at a time, one layer at a time. This friend's tenderness, encouragement, and listening were like a soothing balm to my heart. So if you need to cry over your pain from the past, do it. It will truly help in your healing. When we don't allow ourselves the opportunity to cry, we are stuffing our pain deeper inside of us. That makes it harder to heal and takes longer to heal.

Some people suggested that I needed to be more outgoing, so I tried. It didn't fit; I was just not an outgoing person. God didn't build me that way. In public, when I ran into someone I knew, and we spoke, my voice came out in a whisper. Sometimes not at all. Just my mouth moving. In time, I learned that it's okay to be the way I am. I decided that God made me this way. So if that's okay with Him, it's okay with me. I am not as introverted as I was, though I am a loner. I don't know if that's because of my upbringing or if it's completely natural. But I'm fine as is. I still don't often speak out, even in a small group of friends, even those I fully trust. Sometimes I feel like I should speak out in a group setting, but then I seek another opinion, second-guessing myself. If I truly believe the Lord is prompting me to speak or to share, I usually hesitate, but I do try to say what He is directing me to say. Even now, I guess that I still judge what it is that I intend to say and if it has merit.

It can be exciting and strange to learn about this person who lived inside of you but was not allowed to be free. You'll find out that this person isn't as bad as you were led to believe. You might even like her! Praise God! When I first started renewing my mind, I felt like trusting that I was "the apple of God's eye" was being prideful and presumptuous. But His word reveals how valued we are to the Creator of the universe, even me, even you. And as I said earlier, God *cannot* lie.

When I think back to the days of my childhood and youth, there is no longer any pain. The memories are fading. The dreaded dreams have ended. The physical pain I endured isn't even a sting now. The critical, negative words are all being replaced by God's opinion of me; I am fearfully and wonderfully made; I am the apple of His eye. The emotional pain has been soothed by the "Balm of Gilead." Remembering my father doesn't cause me to cringe and revive the bitterness and resentment. The tears no longer come. All that's left is a regret that things were the way they were, a sadness of what could have been but was not. Now as I think about my father, I remember the good qualities about him. Yes, he had some good qualities. He was a very, very hard worker. Whatever he worked at, he worked with integrity. Our house was extremely well maintained, the yard pristine. Even my mother's roses were very well cared for by my father. He was gracious, kind, and patient to everyone he came in contact with—family or strangers. Strange that I brought out the worst in him.

It now has been thirty-six years since my first deliverance. Time and the Lord's healing and restoration have healed me almost completely. Almost. Mostly what's left is sadness that things were the way they were for both my father and me. Today, I can honestly say that now I feel a tenderness for him and deep regret for what could have been a very good father-and-daughter relationship. Dare I say it? Yes, I do love my father. I love him because of the kind of person I've learned to see through healed eyes and heart. I committed many years ago to show him mercy. It didn't come easy or quickly. A little mercy never hurt anyone—the receiver or the giver.

> Therefore, be merciful just as your Father (in heaven) also is merciful. (Luke 6:36 NKJV)

> Blessed are the merciful, for they shall obtain mercy. (the Beatitudes found in Matthew 5:7 NKJV)

> For judgment is without mercy to one
> who has shown no mercy. Mercy triumphs
> over judgment. (James 2:13 NKJV)

God has mercy on us even as sinners in the giving of His Son and many, many blessings, so how dare we not have mercy on those who sin against us? (I do realize that there are survivors of extreme abuse who want to show no mercy. I believe in God's eyes mercy is not required, only forgiveness.)

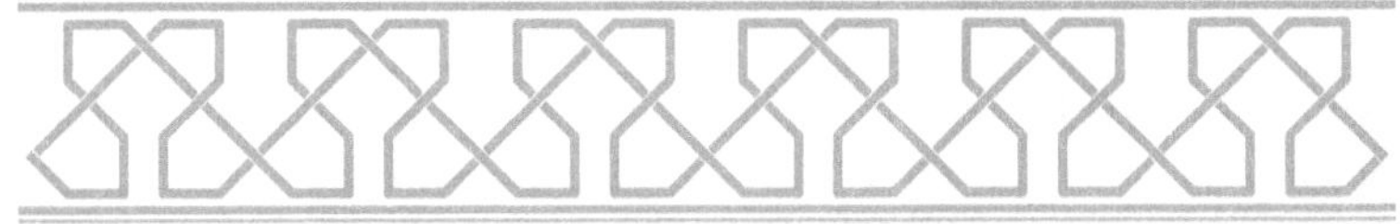

A New Calling

A FEW YEARS ago, I was on my computer—I don't recall what I was doing—but I was listening to Christian music. A song that I had never heard before, but was a few years old, began. It was called "Alabaster Box." As I listened to it, I heard the Lord say, "The alabaster box is your heart." For reasons unknown to me at that time, I started writing about our hearts being alabaster boxes. (Alabaster is a natural stone similar to marble but softer than marble and can be found in many countries, in many colors and veining. Some stone is even translucent. As with marble, alabaster can be carved but not used as kitchen or bathroom counters because of its *soft* nature.) In God's Word, there are stories about two women and their alabaster boxes. They each refer to a woman who breaks open her literal alabaster box, filled with *nard*, and pours out the oil onto Jesus to bless Him and anoint Him. (*Nard* is a very costly, very fragrant perfume from the *spikenard* plant.)

I approached my co-pastor and said, "I think God has given me a word to share." She has known me many, many years.

Her reply was, "I'm not surprised you have a word. I'm surprised that you want to share it."

A few weeks later, I shared it with my small church (in a very shaky voice). *Me. The mentally challenged, unwanted, bad-to-the-core, third daughter*, sharing a word with a group of my peers. What would my father have said? "Don't attempt it, you'll fail." "What do you have to say that anyone would want to hear?" (I can hear him say that right now.) Or, maybe, since our deliverance experience, "Wow, My, good for you!" This woman who carried inferiority and fear with her for almost a lifetime was speaking in a formal setting. The Lord must have been satisfied because He's given me a word to share several times since then. I'm *always* nervous, but I feel so blessed that God chose me to share a word that He gave, and in a regular church service, no doubt, not with just a few close friends.

One of the words the Lord gave me to share later on was about forgiving and forgetting. I elaborated on it earlier. Having gone through *forgiving* and *forgetting* allowed me to be able to teach on the subject. Praise God. You must do both. If we have the right attitude and a pure heart, as God desires for us (not a perfect heart), we'll treat others the way we want to be treated. Let it go, and let God heal and revive your broken heart, your wounded spirit. It's hard to let go of the pain and bitterness and resentment. And the memories. But it is *essential* that we do. Complete healing and recovery will not come without forgiving and forgetting. Only then will the person *inside*, the person God created us to be, come forth and be able to fulfill the calling and accomplish the mandate and the assignment that God placed on us at or even before our conception.

My life is not perfect. I am not perfectly whole; I still get nervous when God gives me a word to share, but hope-fully, the real me, the person God created in my body, will be released this side of heaven. The important thing is that I am no longer in bondage to demonic forces. I may realize that I need more deliverance, but it's been freedom each time for me, so I'm open to it. Are you? And after deliverance comes our own resurrection, a rehabilitation inside, a renewal of who we are deep inside, takes place. As I've said, I am not a part of the mental/emotional health community. I'm just one of many Christians who have been tormented by demonic forces and now have been set free and healed on the inside. Praise God!

Last year, I shared my testimony with my church. I believe that sharing my story brought a great deal of healing to me. It was the hardest thing I ever did. I sobbed all the way through it, but my church was patient and loving toward me, and I pulled through it. When I remember the whacks to my backside now, there is no more pain. I can no longer feel the sting of the slaps to my backside or to my face. The cruel words now are very, very distant and becoming unfamiliar to me. I recognize now that I feel more freedom to be what, how, and who God intended me to be. I never felt like a whole person; I felt like I was defective. But God and His healing and restorative power through Jesus Christ have reversed that. I've learned that it's okay to be me and that I'm not all the things my father spoke of me. I believe that as I share my testimony and my story, more healing will come until more healing is no longer needed. It's amazing what a difference sharing your story can make in your life and aid in your healing. Please know that what God has done for me, dear friend, He can do for you.

Do you need inner healing? Are you suffering from deep-seated pain that controls your life? Do disturbing dreams torment your sleep? Do crushing memories cloud your mind and disable you? The blood of Jesus and His broken body paid for our healing and our restoration. Jesus gave Himself, willingly, so that we would have life and life more abundantly. If there is one scripture that explains the Bible and describes God's love for us, it's Isaiah 61:1. It reads,

> The Spirit of the Lord God is upon Me; Because the Lord has anointed Me to preach good news to the poor (in spirit). He has sent Me to heal the broken-hearted; to proclaim liberty to the captives and the opening of the prison to those who are bound.

This scripture says it all. There really isn't more to say. Inner healing comes after deliverance. You can't have healing first because the demonic spirits that torment you and control you won't allow it. It's like a physical ailment—you must deal with the infection, with the disease, before healing can come to your body. It's the same principle.

If you believe or wonder if you need deliverance, look for a Spirit-filled church that practices deliverance. You may be able to find a deliverance ministry, even a lay deliverance ministry, like the women who ministered to me. They exist for your benefit. They don't care how you got into bondage except to get information that would help shed light on how they should minister to you. Any truth will set us free. How much more *the* truth—Jesus Christ—the name above all names?

While writing this manuscript, I told the Lord that a lot of memories had faded. I couldn't recall them all. He replied, "This book isn't about abuse. It's about deliverance." Always remember, there is nothing so *big* that God *can't* handle it and nothing so *small* that He *won't* handle it.

Salvation Is Easy

Do you know Jesus? Have you been saved from your sins? It's easy to be saved. All you have to do is acknowledge that you are a sinner and that you need Jesus to save you for you to go to heaven for your eternal life and then ask Him to save you. He won't say no. He won't refuse you. Some denominations use the ABC approach: *Acknowledge* that you are a sinner. *Believe* that God sent His Son to die on a cross to save you from your sins. *Confess* Jesus as your Lord and Savior. (He has to be *Lord* before He can be *Savior* because He has to be in a high position to become your Savior.) Here is a simple prayer:

"Heavenly Father, I know that I am a sinner and I need Jesus to save me from my sins. I believe that Jesus is the Savior of the world, sent by God, who died on the cross to pay for my sins so that I don't have to. I'm asking You, Father, to forgive me of all my sins and that Jesus come into my heart as my Lord and my Savior. I ask in the *name* of Jesus."

You always pray to God in *Jesus's name*.

If you pray this prayer, I'll see you in heaven someday.

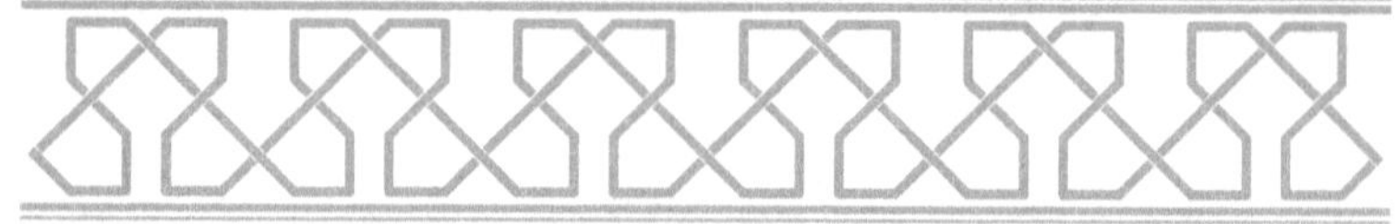

Aaronic Blessing

The Lord bless you and keep you
Oh, the Lord make His face shine upon
you and be gracious to you
The Lord lift up His countenance upon you
And give you His peace
—Numbers 6:24–26 NKJV

About the Author

MYRA WAS A victim of child abuse. Now she is a victorious survivor, having been delivered of oppression and tormenting memories, and healed of emotional wounds through the power of Jesus Christ. She is a still life painter in oils and writes poetry. During cold months, she quilts. On occasion, she shares a word that God has given her with her church. She is a widow, having been married for fifty-one years. Her son, daughter-in-law, and granddaughter live in Saskatchewan, Canada. Viewing the northern lights in person is on Myra's bucket list.